# PREPARING TO TACK

# PREPARING TO TACK

## When Physicians Change Careers

## Jack Kushner,
### M.D., M.G.A., FACS, FICS

Authors Choice Press
Bloomington

# Preparing to Tack
## When Physicians Change Careers

Authors Choice Press
an imprint of iUniverse, Inc.

iUniverse books may be ordered through booksellers or by contacting:

iUniverse
1663 Liberty Drive
Bloomington, IN 47403
www.iuniverse.com
1-800-Authors (1-800-288-4677)

Because of the dynamic nature of the Internet, any web addresses or links contained in
this book may have changed since publication and may no longer be valid. The views
expressed in this work are solely those of the author and do not necessarily reflect the
views of the publisher, and the publisher hereby disclaims any responsibility for them.

Any people depicted in stock imagery provided by Thinkstock are models,
and such images are being used for illustrative purposes only.

Certain stock imagery © Thinkstock.

ISBN: 978-1-4502-9314-3 (sc)

Printed in the United States of America

iUniverse rev. date: 03/23/2011

To my parents, Rose and Louis H. Kushner;
to my wife, Annetta;
and to my daughters, Reyna and Eve

# Contents

# Acknowledgments

I wish to thank Ms. Geraldine Brooks and Ms. Eve Kushner for their editorial assistance.

# PREPARING TO TACK

# Chapter 1
# The Last Straw

In August 1994, as I watched the Senate debate health care on C-Span, I decided to leave medicine. Sen. Nancy Kassebaum from Kansas was on the Senate floor, explaining how the Mitchell bill would control our lives. For example, the bill would mandate balanced practices according to governmental standards. This meant that my neurosurgical practice should have a certain proportion of Caucasians, Blacks, Asians, and Hispanics. If my practice did not measure up to these newly instituted criteria, I might very well be assigned to practice community medicine in the inner cities of Baltimore or Washington, each an hour's drive from my home in Annapolis, Maryland.

More bureaucratic snafus? I couldn't believe it. Just that week I had jumped through my share of hoops. One of my patients, a thirty-eight-year-old woman, had had a positive CAT scan of the brain and a positive MRI. These tests showed her to have a lesion in her frontal lobe that was giving her headaches, lethargy, seizures, confusion, and motor weakness on the opposite side of her body. I wanted to administer further diagnostic studies. To do this, I needed approval from this patient's HMO. The person on the other end of the line had never examined my patient. Nevertheless, she explained to me that the HMO would not authorize either a stereotactic brain biopsy or an open craniotomy to remove this brain lesion because the radiologist who performed the CAT scan and MRI felt that they probably indicated a malignant lesion such as a glioblastoma multiforme. She said if it were indeed a malignancy, it would not be cost-effective for the HMO to pay for further treatment. She added that many radiology textbooks assert that the radiologist can usually make definitive diagnoses of malignant tumors from such tests. I countered that it was imperative that we obtain a tissue diagnosis, but the HMO employee would not yield. Out of desperation I wrote to my senators, my congressman, and the insurance commissioner. Finally, they allowed me to proceed with further diagnostic studies. A craniotomy revealed a treatable tuberculoma, rather than a malignancy. As of yet, I have received no apology from the HMO. To my knowledge, they have not changed their policy.

The same week, another HMO notified me that they refused to pay any hospital bills for a forty-eight-year-old man I was treating. They maintained that he did not have a life-threatening disease and was admitted as an emergency. It is true that I initially saw this man in the emergency room at the Anne Arundel Medical Center in Annapolis, Maryland, when he was convulsing. After his seizures came under control, I requested a CAT scan of the brain, which the radiologist interpreted as showing a possible cerebral aneurysm. We transferred the patient by helicopter to a tertiary medical facility, Washington Hospital Center, where he had cerebral angiography, which failed to reveal any aneurysm. Initially, the patient remained lethargic, but in a few days he perked up. Nothing further was done. He was diagnosed as having idiopathic epilepsy without there being any discernible cause, and he was discharged on anticonvulsant medication.

I wrote letters to senators about my frustration with

2

how the HMO handled this case and how irresponsibly many HMOs are acting. I advised against imposing a system of health care on us that would center around these HMOs. These letters were returned to me, stating that I should refer this matter to the proper authorities. Thus far, there has been no response from the insurance commissioner.

In the same week, I spent hours on the telephone arguing with another HMO. I had just removed a tumor from a fifty-year-old patient. I had done the operation in the Washington Hospital Center. After an uneventful recovery, I transferred him out of the ICU and four days later wanted to transfer him back to Annapolis, where he originated. The family also wanted him transferred, but the HMO supervisor said she couldn't be responsible if something happened to him in the ambulance. I explained that I would be the responsible person for the transfer and that I had been practicing medicine in this manner for years. Only after I advised her that the HMO might be in violation of the federal antidumping law, which says that no one can obstruct a patient or a patient's family from returning to the originating hospital if there are no medical contraindications, did we finally receive authorization to transfer the patient. I believe the law was written to protect those patients who are transferred for medical reasons, but whose return might be jeopardized by a lack of insurance. It might be expensive to litigate this question just to find out whether it applies to HMO patients.

In the same week, right after I did a spinal fusion on a patient, I received a phone call from his HMO. The HMO wanted to know when I was planning to discharge the patient. I informed the HMO employee that the patient had just come out of the operating room into the recovery room and that I wasn't certain how long he would stay. She then told me that she was authorizing only two days of hospital stay, and that it would be necessary for me to call her back for any additional days of coverage.

I have had enough. These events, along with all the other headaches I have already faced, have convinced me to leave medicine. Although I have yet to set the date, I intend to change careers. I have researched my options and have a roadmap with which to start out on a new trail.

# Chapter 2

# Why I Chose
# Medicine in the First Place

Ever since I was a kid, I wanted to go into medicine. I was born in 1939 and grew up on National Avenue in Montgomery, Alabama. Six families had a crop of boys between them, and we formed tight friendships. A few medical emergencies threatened to separate us, though, and alerted me to the importance of medical knowledge. Once, in 1946, while we were playing hide-and-seek in our bare feet, Hilton Starr stepped on a steak bone that a dog had partially buried. His father, Sgt. Ben Starr, who had just returned from the Pacific theater, soaked Hilton's foot in a washbasin full of water under the weeping willow tree in their front yard. Blood gushed out and everyone gathered around to see how Sergeant Starr would stop the hemorrhaging. With a tourniquet, he did just that. Unfortunately, Hilton's problems did not stop there. He developed tetanus, and although he was taken to the hospital at Maxwell Field, he died about two weeks later of what was called "lockjaw."

For a while afterward we all wore shoes, and eventually we were inoculated against tetanus. Even today the treatment of full-blown tetanus is daunting, and prevention is the best form of therapy. Clostridium tetanus infects its victims and releases an endotoxin that causes tetanic muscular contraction. Patients usually suffer muscular spasms, hyperthermia, and convulsions, and many die, although some patients have been successfully treated with different regimens.

Approximately two months after Hilton's death, his older brother Bart was carried home unconscious in the arms of Joe Van Wezel. Bart had been standing on his bicycle seat while riding and had fallen off. He was taken to the hospital at Maxwell Field. Although I was only six years old, I remember people talking about a cerebral concussion or contusion and about the development of a subdural or epidural hematoma. Because there was no neurosurgeon at Maxwell, there was talk about transferring Bart to Nashville, Tennessee, or having a neurosurgeon travel to Montgomery to see him.

There are different degrees of head injuries. The least severe is called a cerebral concussion, which is a transitory disruption of cerebral function due entirely to trauma. During the traumatic event, the brain moves, and this movement makes the brain accelerate. This strain is significant, but it does not produce structural damage as is seen in a cerebral contusion. This injury is transitory and may be only of momentary importance. Usually, a full recovery can be anticipated.

A cerebral contusion is a more serious brain injury and is most often caused by a localizing injury to the skull that strikes and compresses the brain to such an extent that it injures the cerebral tissue itself. The brain may be injured by other immobile objects within the cranial cavity, such as the tentorium or the petrous ridge. These patients may be unconscious for a period of time, and ones with serious injuries can die. Skull fractures can also cause cerebral contusions. A great deal of progress has been made in treating these closed-head injuries, but most do not require surgery. They do require intensive-care monitoring, constant ventricular fluid-pressure monitoring, and cerebral perfusion-pressure controls.

Blood clots can appear in the subdural space or the epidural space. Usually epidural space bleeding is arterial in origin and should be evacuated on an emergency basis or the patient will die shortly. Subdural hematomas are not quite as urgent, but acute subdural hematomas are associated with a high mortality rate from the associated cerebral contusion. Subacute and chronic subdural hematomas have to be evacuated, and many patients have a good result after treatment.

Bart indeed had a contusion and could have died. Instead, he went on to make an excellent recovery. Many will recognize him as the Green Bay Packers' quarterback who was the Most Valuable Player in the 1967 Super Bowl.

Three more of our close friends and playmates were killed in a car accident. Losing so many friends did much to impress matters of life and death on me at an early age. I wanted to enhance life and delay death, a passion that played a significant role in my career choice.

Besides the impact of such events on my career, I was influenced by my environment and relationships. While I was in junior high school, Bill Dobbins, an older friend, extolled the virtues of being a country doctor. He used to talk to us about being the only doctor in a semirural area like Montgomery and how one could really help a lot of patients. Bill used to say that a country doctor has a distinct advantage. After he is called to see a patient, he can think about the diagnosis and his course of action while driving to the patient's house. Bill never became a country doctor; instead, he became a professor of gastroenterology at the University of Michigan.

Later on I befriended Bill Dismukes at Baldwin Junior

High School, Camp Rotary, and Lanier High School. I would meet Bill again at medical school in Birmingham. I cannot say exactly in what way his friendship exerted a positive influence on my decision to enter medicine, but I believe to this day that his path in life influenced mine. I think it was because he was a peer that he was able to leave such a strong impression on me. Today he is professor of infectious diseases at the University of Alabama in Birmingham.

Dr. Sol Selikoff was another role model for me. He took care of our family for many years. He talked to me about medicine and would later take me on rounds with him at St. Margaret's hospital and encourage me to enter medicine. While I was in the seventh grade we discussed my school courses and he encouraged me to write to the registrar at the University of Alabama Medical School to see whether or not I should take Latin. Ms. Virginia Baxley, in 1952, wrote me a letter saying that while Latin was no longer absolutely essential to gain admission to medical school, she encouraged me to take it because so few applicants had a background in Latin and she considered it helpful. In 1964, she returned to me my original letter of inquiry. She said she knew that one day I would be graduating, so she had saved that letter all those years.

My parents were always very supportive. My father went with me twice to see Robert Mitchum in the movie *Not As a Stranger,* which was about medicine and medical school. Even when I was a youngster, he talked about how he would help me set up an office and get started in medicine. I really needed my parents' encouragement when I came home from Tulane University my freshman year thinking I was failing every course. As my father put me back on the plane that Sunday night, he told me that if things didn't work out at school, I could always come back to his grocery store in Montgomery and work with him. I had worked in his store on many weekends and summer holidays and knew for certain that I had to find a way out of that situation. Just thinking of that awful option inspired me to work harder whenever I felt discouraged.

While I was a student at the University of Sheffield in Sheffield, England, the University of Alabama notified me that I had been accepted to medical school. Shortly afterward, I heard the same news from Tulane Medical School. After much deliberation I chose Alabama and felt fortunate for the education I acquired, for my medical training and experiences, and for the people I met. It was in Birmingham that I met Dr. Galbraith, Dr. Harsh, Dr. Humphrey, and Dr. Elizabeth Crosby.

Although other neurosurgeons also taught at the medical school, it was Dr. Galber Galbraith and Dr. Griffin Harsh who inspired me to go into neurosurgery. Dr. T. Humphrey taught neuroanatomy and introduced me to Dr. Elizabeth Crosby, who commuted from Ann Arbor, Michigan, when she was the professor of neuroanatomy. I would later have contact with Dr. Crosby again when I was at the University of Michigan.

At that time, I won a chance to study tropical medicine at the Gorgas Laboratory in Panama. This would prove to be important, because I studied tropical diseases firsthand at Gorgas and would later use that education and experience in Vietnam. It was while I was in Panama that I developed a meaningful correspondence with a woman named Annetta Horwitz. We would marry when I graduated from medical school.

After I finished my studies at the University of Alabama School of Medicine, several more people influenced my decision to become a neurosurgeon. As an intern at the George Washington University Hospital, I worked with Dr.

Hugo Rizzoli and was impressed with his demeanor, his compassion, and his neurosurgical skills. I only worked with him occasionally as a surgical intern, but later as a practicing neurosurgeon in Annapolis I would work with him over twenty years. Dr. Rizzoli was one of the last residents to work with Dr. Walter Dandy, a founder of neurosurgery at the Johns Hopkins Hospital. Dr. Rizzoli did a great deal of neurosurgery during World War II and worked with Dr. Barnes Woodhall and Dr. Glen Spurling at Walter Reed Army Medical Center. He served on the American Board of Neurosurgery and as professor of neurosurgery at George Washington University, and was awarded the prestigious Humanitarian Award by the American Association of Neurological Surgeons.

When I served a year as an assistant resident in general surgery at the University of Michigan, I met Dr. Edgar Kahn, professor of neurosurgery. Some say the book and movie *Magnificent Obsession* were all about Dr. Kahn, who encouraged me to go into neurosurgery. Dr. Kahn inspired so many medical students. His presence at the conferences made a great difference. He could talk about diseases with such enthusiasm. He loved to have Dr. Elizabeth Crosby at the conference, and the two of them would make neurosurgery and neuroanatomy come alive. When Dr. Kahn heard that I was going to Vietnam, he paged me several times to assist him personally in surgery. He wanted to be sure that I knew how to drill burr holes, do a subtemporal decompression, and turn a craniotomy flap. He corresponded with me when I was in Vietnam and asked me to come back to Michigan when I finished my military obligation.

Ann Arbor, Michigan, was a hotbed of antiwar sentiment and demonstrations while I was there. There was a great deal of political activity. But it was in that very environment that I decided I really wanted to go to Vietnam as a combat surgeon. This decision became a reality when I received orders to go to Fort Belvoir, Virginia, for part of my service and to Greenland for the rest. Not wishing to go to Greenland, I volunteered to go to Vietnam by writing the Pentagon and President Johnson—unbeknownst to my wife. One day she received a letter from the president of the United States commending me for my patriotism and stating that orders would be forthcoming. Even though twenty-eight years have elapsed, she still feels upset that I volunteered to go to Vietnam without discussing it with her, leaving her and our six-month-old daughter to face the vagaries of life. Shortly after I arrived in Vietnam, my wife sent me an article stating that Arlington Cemetery was full. She wanted to know where the "war hero" wanted to go if he got killed.

Upon arriving in Vietnam, I was assigned to the Sixth Convalescent Center at Cam Rahn Bay. This was where most malaria patients were treated before returning to duty. Only a few of our patients with cerebral malaria died; most of the patients had vivax malaria, which is a less serious form of the disease, and were returned to duty.

Six weeks later I went to Tuy Hoa where the semi-mobile 91st Evacuation Hospital was set up. Col. John Maier, a radiotherapist from Walter Reed Hospital, was the commanding officer. Maj. Ray Smith was the administrative officer, and Col. Estelle Skadova was the nursing supervisor. I had been with the 91st Evacuation Hospital since its formative days at Fort Polk, Louisiana. After we set up, we were protected by the Korean army and the Fourth Infantry as well as an airborne unit. The air base was just up the beach a few miles.

Initially, most of the patients were Vietnamese. Later on, we would have a mixture of Vietnamese and American soldiers. We saw many sorts of injuries, including gunshot wounds to all areas of the body, as well as mine and explosive wounds. I remember exploring lots of abdomens, closing a lot of intestinal holes, resecting a lot of bowel, repairing peripheral vessels, performing amputations, and doing delayed primary closures. I had had two years of surgical training, but I was functioning at a much higher level in large part due to the help and influence of Tom Murphy, who is now a cardiac surgeon in Chicago. I have long felt that surgeons are the only ones who win in a combat situation. Combat surgeons are entrusted with severely injured youngsters who need a doctor's skill and compassion. This is medicine at its purest, without the interference of third parties, such as insurance companies, HMOs, or the government. On one occasion, though, I did face such interference. Once, after I had been up for two nights straight, I received a communication from someone at MACV Headquarters in Saigon criticizing the brevity of my histories and physicals, which usually had on them "GSW to the abdomen," meaning gunshot wound to the abdomen. Because of the large patient load, I rarely saw the need to investigate the patients' family histories, nor did I record much of anything. I wrote back that if they pursued the war in this manner, insisting on detailed paperwork, we would certainly lose the war.

While in Vietnam, I enjoyed going on "Medcap" trips. We would go to a Vietnamese village to win the "hearts and minds" of the people. I treated them with iron and vitamins and gave them medication for their intestinal parasites. The experience gained from my time in Panama was most helpful with this project.

People often ask me if we ever saw any hostile action ourselves. A few times there was a red alert, meaning that Vietcong infiltrators were in the compound. On Sunday

12

evenings, toward the end of my tour, we received some incoming fire that penetrated the tin quonset huts in which we operated. Sometimes it was difficult to identify the enemy. The maid who cleaned our bunks was killed in our compound when she tried to infiltrate and place a mine.

I did not do much in the way of neurosurgery in Vietnam. Our hospital was on the front lines, and we did not have the luxury of doing specialized work. There were no fully trained neurosurgeons with us. Most of the neurosurgical cases were evacuated elsewhere, if they survived. The general surgery and the critical-care management contributed significantly to my education and training.

# Chapter 3
# Dr. Eben Alexander

The most influential person in my professional life has been Dr. Eben Alexander. I first met him when I was an intern at George Washington University. Annetta and I flew to Winston-Salem, North Carolina, for an interview and as a result of that meeting I have had a close personal relationship with him for almost thirty years. His influence has been so pivotal to my thinking, my career, and my life that I will speak at length about him.

The Bowman Gray School of Medicine at Wake Forest University in Winston-Salem, North Carolina, was indeed fortunate to welcome Dr. Alexander to its staff in 1949. Born in Knoxville, Tennessee, he received his undergraduate education at the University of North Carolina and then went on to Harvard Medical School. From there he served a surgical internship at the Peter Bent Brigham Hospital and did his neurosurgical residency at the Children's Hospital in Boston. After five years of study under Dr. Frank Ingraham in Boston, he then went on to Toronto, where he worked under Dr. Ken McKenzie. His neurosurgical training was interrupted for four years when he served in the United States Army at Walter Reed Medical Center and with the armed forces in the South Pacific and Tokyo, for which he was awarded the Bronze Star.

Shortly after Dr. Alexander's arrival in Winston-Salem,

the Bowman Gray School of Medicine appointed him assistant professor of surgery in charge of neurosurgery. In 1954, he was named head of surgery and was appointed professor of surgery, a position he would hold for the next thirty years. From the start, Dr. Alexander became an active member of the hospital and teaching staffs. He solidified his position within the medical school and within the hospital by participating in intramural committee works, such as the committee to study the disposition of the Graylyn Mansion of the Reynolds family as a psychiatric hospital, the search committee for the department chief of audiovisual resources, the Bowman Gray Foundation Board of Trustees, and Executive Committee (where he was the chief of professional services), and the search committee for the chief of the radiology department. He was also on the Liaison Committee with City Hospital to study the feasibility of combining resources. In 1961, he served on the search committee for the department chief of neurology, on the Long-Range Planning Committee, and on the Medical Center Advisory Council. In 1965, he was appointed to the medical center investigation of the Wesley Nursing Home in Charlotte, North Carolina. He was an active member of the ad hoc search committee for department chief of anesthesia in 1966. He was elected to the Surgical Council at the Bowman Gray School of Medicine from 1968–78 and he served on the Joint Administration Board of the North Carolina Baptist Hospital–Bowman Gray Medical Center. He served on the Wake Forest University Senate from 1974 to 1982 and was on the Honorary Degree Committee at Wake Forest University in 1975. Although he stepped down as chief of neurosurgery in 1977, he served as the chairman of the Recognition Protocol Committee. In 1981, he was elected to the senate committee to study the future of the university.

On the national level, Dr. Alexander served on the editorial board of the *Journal of Neurosurgery*, was appointed its chairman from 1969 to 1970, and has been on the advisory board from 1970 to the present. In 1964, he became the editor of the neurosurgical techniques section of the *Journal of Neurosurgery*. He was a consultant to the *Journal of the American Medical Association* from 1965 to 1967. He was an associate editor for *Surgical Neurology* from 1980 to 1985 and was appointed its editor in 1986. In 1980, he was named editor of *The Neurosurgeon* by the American Academy of Neurological Surgery.

He has served as a consultant to the Veterans' Administration Regional Office in Winston-Salem, North Carolina, as well as in Oteen and Swannanoa, North Carolina. In addition, he has been a consultant to the Holston Valley Community Hospital in Kingsport, Tennessee, the Veterans' Administration Hospital in Salisbury, North Carolina, and the Northern Hospital of Surrey County in Mt. Airy, North Carolina. Throughout his forty-year career, he has been honored as a visiting professor at thirty different hospital and medical centers in the United States and in foreign countries from Canada to Thailand.

Dr. Alexander officiated at numerous medical committees on the local and national level: the United Research Foundation of North Carolina in 1958, the Board of Scientific Counselors for the National Institute of Neurological Diseases and Blindness from 1961 to 1964, the Neurological Science Research Training Committee for the National Institute of Neurological Diseases and Blindness from 1962 to 1966, the Advisory Committee for the Clinical Neurology Information Center, the Council of Medical Specialty Societies in 1976, the Graduate Medical Education Committee in 1980, and the National Board of Medical Examiners. In 1984, he was on the North Carolina Board of

Medical Examiners. Since 1984, he has served as chairman of the committee on Ethics at the Bowman Gray School of Medicine. From 1959 to 1962, he participated in the cooperative study of Intracranial Aneurysms and Acute Subarachnoid Hemorrhage. From 1968 to 1980, he contributed to the Brain Tumor Study Group for the National Cancer Institute.

At eighty-one years of age, Dr. Alexander remains active in neurosurgical research and writing, studying the proper placement of shunts for patients suffering from hydrocephalus and the optimum time for their revision; evaluating the role of subtemporal decompression in the treatment of intracranial pressure, whether from trauma or infected shunts; carrying on an ongoing study to evaluate the use of acrylic, wire, and a new style of clips in posterior cervical fusions; and finally, evaluating the treatment of spondylolisthesis without pars defects.

He has been recognized for his leadership ability on the national level. He was elected to the American Academy of Neurological Surgery in 1950, has served as its secretary-treasurer, vice president, and president, and still serves on the Executive Committee. He was elected president of the Society of Neurological Surgeons. He is a member of the American Association for the Advancement of Science, the American Medical Association, the Council of Medical Education, and the Liaison Committee on Medical Education. He was elected to the American Association of Neurological Surgeons and has served as its secretary, treasurer, and president. He has also sat on the Executive Committee and on the Council of State Neurosurgical Societies. He was elected as a Fellow to the American College of Surgeons and served as vice president from 1976 to 1977.

Furthermore, he holds membership in the American Surgical Association, the Association of American Medical

Colleges, the Congress of Neurological Surgeons, the Harvard Medical Alumni Association, the International Society of Pediatric Neurosurgery, the Massachusetts Medical Society, the North Carolina Medical Society, the National Board of Medical Examiners, and the Neurosurgical Society of America, of which he was vice president. He has also served on various committees for the North Carolina Medical Society, the North Carolina Surgical Association, and the Section of Cerebrovascular Surgery for the American Association of Neurological Surgeons.

Over the years he has received many honors. In 1969, he received the Door-Opener Award from the Mayor's Commission on Employment for the Handicapped of Winston-Salem. In 1958, he received the Hadassah Humanitarian Award in Winston-Salem. In 1969, the Governor's Commission on Employment of the Handicapped in North Carolina selected him Physician of the Year. In 1980, he was the honored guest at the annual meeting of the Congress of Neurological Surgeons. In 1984, he received the Cushing Award for Outstanding Service from the American Association of Neurological Surgeons. In 1989, he was honored with the Distinguished Service Award, Society of Neurological Surgeons.

Dr. Alexander generously gave of his time and energy to the community at large. Over the years, he has served as medical adviser for the North Carolina Paraplegic Association and as president of the Rotary Club of Winston-Salem. He has held seats on the Board of Directors for the United Fund of Forsyth County, the Board of the Chamber of Commerce of Winston-Salem, and the Medical Advisory Committee for Goodwill Industries. He was appointed chairman of the Committee for Worship for the Centenary United Methodist Church and chairman for the Arts Fund Drive for Physicians of Forsyth County. He presently serves on the Medical Advisory Committee for the Triad United Methodist Home. Over the past forty years, he has contributed ten chapters to various medical textbooks, published 125 articles in medical journals, and has written numerous editorials, letters, and abstracts.

Dr. Alexander could inspire and empower his residents to do all sorts of things. He believed that the glue holding the entire neurosurgical department together was the resident staff he had selected for training. He was able to teach by example and by demonstration. I was asked to assist him on a lumbar disc operation when I first started residency. Throughout the operation, Dr. Alexander pointed out the nerve root, the ligament, the dura, and finally the large ruptured disc. When I left the operating room I felt that I had seen the most exciting disc operation ever to have been performed because Dr. Alexander made it appear that way. Since that time, I have operated on hundreds and hundreds of ruptured discs, but never have I seen one as exciting as the one we removed that day. Once I saw a patient in the outpatient clinic with hydrocephalus and a myelomeningocele. Dr. Alexander examined the patient and asked me what I thought about the case. I remarked that the patient had a myelomeningocele and hydrocephalus and that there was not a great deal to talk about. Dr. Alexander spent forty-five minutes talking to the patient and to me. He encouraged me to research these problems, which eventually led me to deliver a research paper at a major neurosurgical organization.

All the residents thought Dr. Alexander had a great deal of charisma and sought to emulate him. He was an effective leader who was able to influence others to attain goals. He possessed power over us, but he did not need to exert it because it was not his personal style. He challenged his subordinates on a more intellectual level by using his expertise and knowledge. His residents were assigned interesting and desirable tasks as well as greater responsibility for patients. Through these leadership devices he was able to facilitate their career development and mold them into capable neurosurgeons.

# Chapter 4
# Why Doctors Are Frustrated

At first, the rally went smoothly. Several doctors stood up before the crowd and talked about the need for health care reform in view of the economic climate. Other physicians expressed concern for their patients and the 38 million Americans with no health insurance. Predictably, one of the state senators appeared and said that he was mainly interested in the welfare of his constituents and that he had tried to be fair in debating the bill to cap physicians' incomes. About this time some doctor in the audience yelled out, "What about all the times we go to the emergency room in the middle of the night? Have you taken all of this into consideration?" The state senator castigated the crowd and said he would no longer try to mollify doctors. The crowd dispersed, but some of the doctors went directly to the offices of key senators. As a result of this personal interaction, a compromise health care reform bill was passed later in the legislative session allowing the doctors input on the fee structure that the state would set in the next five years.

The rally typified the health care revolution sweeping the nation. Historians can draw parallels between the effects of the industrial revolution on the workplace and the health care revolution on the patient-doctor relationship. Ever since the health care issue played a key role in the

Pennsylvania senatorial election in November 1992, the morale in the American medical community has deteriorated. Indeed, shortly after the rally occurred near Maryland's state capitol building, practicing physicians lost enthusiasm about the future of their careers. Maryland physicians have made an annual ritual of gathering in Lawyers' Alley to petition their grievances to the state legislature. They feel that this annual event is necessary to discourage legislators from passing destructive health care laws and to encourage them to pass helpful ones. For example, about ten years ago, the doctors urged the legislators to reform malpractice laws. Although the legislature did put a cap on suits for pain and suffering and established arbitration review panels, the malpractice problem remains one of the major scandals in our nation's history.

Conversation in doctor's lounges and cafeterias usually turns to the forthcoming Clinton health care policy changes, which remain uncertain. Recession has devastated industries around the world, including those in the United States, where most citizens obtain their health care insurance through their place of employment. As corporations lay off employees, people lose their health insurance. In addition, health care expenditures in the United States have reportedly reached 14 percent of the gross national product. Forecasters say the expenses could rise to 20 percent of the GNP within the next ten years if present trends continue.

Many physicians feel they are being blamed unfairly for the increase in health care costs. In several polls, Americans see malpractice lawyers as the number-one culprit for escalating health care costs. Hospitals and insurance companies rank right behind them, with doctors in fourth place. Although there is plenty of blame to go around, advanced technology, an aging population, and the lack of patient power and financial participation in medical decisions contribute significantly to the rising cost of health care. Because of the concerted action that many states are taking to control health care costs, physicians, and the practice of medicine, doctors are increasingly thinking the unthinkable: changing careers.

There are so many reasons to leave medicine: the progressive health care revolution that gives all the power to the managed-care insurance companies, the usurpation of physician autonomy, and the replacement of the physician-patient relationship with HMO policies. Many doctors have never considered life after medicine and have made no plans for that time in their future. Despite their ample education, some doctors say, "I don't know how to do anything else. I am trapped in this system and I can't get out. If I knew what else I could do, I would definitely change careers." Some insurance agents report that there has been an increase in the number of physicians filing claims for disability due to depression, largely due to their inability to deal with the changes in the health care delivery system. Many doctors feel that it is too late in their lives to make such a change. However, it is becoming more and more acceptable to switch or modify a medical career. A number of physicians have switched careers successfully without disgrace and have discovered that there is indeed a life after the first career choice—a choice made usually at a very young age, without the benefit of maturity or experience.

According to Balagot, physicians consider leaving the bedside because of disillusionment with medicine, third-party interference, the doctor's own medical problems, financial considerations, threat of increased litigation, and political and economic environmental factors (Balagot, 1992). Other reasons include changing needs, values, and interests, and a desire to make a contribution elsewhere.

Doctors might also leave medicine because of their frustration with HMOs and PPOs. Health Maintenance Organizations and Preferred Provider Organizations are part of managed health care, where a patient enters the system and sees an assigned salaried physician. This "gatekeeper" physician may be paid a commission or given a financial incentive not to perform any diagnostic tests, not to arrange any referrals to a specialist, or not to suggest hospitalization. If, in fact, hospitalization is required, the doctor must seek permission from someone a thousand miles away who has not examined the patient, but is relying on preprinted guidelines to manage the patient. When the doctor receives permission and a precertification number, a specialist must give medical care at a prearranged discount, often at an HMO hospital. The admitting doctor is then told how many hospital days will be allowed and to seek further permission if the patient cannot be discharged within the allotted time. The use of hospital days is reviewed and payment for "unnecessary days" may be denied later. Medical decisions are also evaluated and may be questioned. If the patient files a complaint, fifty of the doctor's cases will be reviewed and audited by the State Physician Quality Assurance Board. A Syrian poet in exile, Nazar Kabany, wrote the following lines: "Would a bird need the permission of the Interior Ministry to fly / and would a fish need a permit to swim / We would live in a world where birds couldn't fly and fish couldn't swim" (Kabany, 1993).

As if all of the above were not enough to cause a certain amount of disillusionment with practicing medicine in America, there is still the threat of litigation. Formerly, a spirit of human cooperation existed in the United States, which was maintained by contracts between parties. Later, a system developed to allocate the cost of accidents among producers of goods and services. There has been a gradual replacement of contractual law by tort law, which has created a litigation free-for-all in the United States (Huber, 1988). Now we have employees pitted against their employers and against insurance companies. Citizens seek damages against fellow citizens, patients are set against their doctors, and some people are hostile to all professionals. The tort courts and juries have set standards for every possible situation where damages may be collected: on ski slopes, in surgery, or in flawed mechanical and architectural designs. Furthermore, over the years the number of tort suits has grown dramatically and the amount awarded by the judges and juries has increased considerably.

More medical malpractice suits were filed from 1977 to 1987 than in the entire history of this country's legal system (Huber, 1988). In addition, more suits have been recorded against cities and the federal government than ever before. It has been estimated that a plaintiff's probability of winning a suit has increased from 20 percent to 50 percent (Huber, 1988).

Today, it costs a physician between $20,000 and $30,000 to defend a malpractice case. Even when a physician has won a malpractice case at arbitration, the plaintiff will often appeal it and insist on a jury trial. The insurance company then pressures the physician to settle the case out of court so that the uncertainty of a jury trial will be minimized for the insurance company, regardless of the case's lack of merit. As a result of this uncertainty, lawyers know that if they sue a physician they will likely come away with a great deal of money, even if the case is without merit. If they win the case, they know that they will come away with an even greater sum.

Doctors have increasingly come to resent government interference in medicine in two areas: limits on national health care spending and on doctors' charges. Some medical organizations now argue that "a physician's right to practice medicine is a property right" protected by the Constitution. Lawyers for the American Medical Association contend: "When price controls are imposed on all physicians, there can be no claim that they have been incurred voluntarily. The only way to avoid controls would be to abandon the practice of medicine entirely. However, physicians make huge investments in specialized training and equipment—an investment which would have no value if not devoted to the practice of medicine. A decision to abandon the profession would completely wipe out this investment" (Pear, 1993).

An additional incentive for physicians to leave medicine is the overall hostility toward physicians and patients that permeates the Clinton health plan. Whatever the original intentions might have been, such as guaranteed universal coverage and "managed competition" (Arnett, 1993), the Health Security Act proposes three penalties for noncompliance. First, all American citizens not exempted must register with a health alliance and must pay the premiums. If an individual, family, or employee fails to pay these premiums, it can result in a fine of $5,000 or three times the amount owed. The government will provide help to the health alliance in hunting down those people who don't pay up. Second, there is an "All-Payer Health Care Fraud and Abuse Control Program." Federal authorities will run this without any revenues appropriated by Congress and will collect its monies from doctors and health plans who commit "health care offenses." Third, the act states that "whoever, in any manner involving a health alliance or health plan," creates or uses any documents that contain false statements can be fined or imprisoned for five years or both. Further decrees state that anyone who acquires services from a health alliance, plan, or provider under false pretenses shall be fined or imprisoned for up to ten years (Arnett, 1993). Things that have been considered patient advocacy in the past may now be considered a federal offense under the Clinton plan. Sometimes doctors try to get their patients earlier surgical dates. If a doctor does this and takes "anything of value"—such as a gift—both the patient and the physician are subject to fines and prison for up to fifteen years. The government can fine doctors and health plans up to $10,000 for not providing what they determine to be proper data on all patient visits. This record-keeping must be in compliance with the newly created Quality Management Council. The government can fine pharmaceutical companies $10,000 a day if they do not provide information quickly enough to satisfy them; if the government later finds an error, they can levy a fine against the pharmaceutical company for $100,000 per violation.

President Clinton continues to tell everyone that they can choose their own doctor with his plan. The fact is that there is a special set of rules that makes it dangerous for any doctor to practice independently or for new doctors to establish their own practice. For example, physicians working on a fee-for-service basis "may collectively negotiate the fee schedule with the regional alliances" (Arnett, 1993). The state may "establish its own statewide fee schedule" that overrides any negotiated rates. Physicians who practice on a fee-for-service basis may not withhold their service regardless of their feeling about the state rate and are prohibited from "engaging in or threatening action to engage in a boycott" (Arnett, 1993). In addition, the negotiated fee schedule can be ignored by the health alliance that exceeds its budget and can withhold any payments to providers to insure that expenditures do not exceed the budget. Any physicians who choose to practice in a single-payer system face "automatic, mandatory, non-discretionary reductions in payments" to allow the state to stay within its budget. If any health plan becomes insolvent, successful health plans and all of their participants can be assessed to make up the difference.

# Chapter 5
# Physicians Have Successfully Switched

It takes a great deal of courage for physicians to admit that, for whatever reason, they are not satisfied with their careers. This can be difficult to face in view of all the effort, study, time, and money they have invested in medicine. Most doctors will face life after medicine anyway when they retire at age sixty-five; those who think of leaving their profession before then are in no way inadequate. Doctors contemplating this change should reflect on their lives and needs, consider the repercussions of a change, and form a strategic plan. Sometimes returning to school gives one more time to collect one's thoughts and make contacts, but it also delays the inevitable decision.

History is replete with examples of doctors who started out in medicine and then went on to enjoy other careers. Although many people are familiar with John Keats's poetry, some may not realize that he actually tried a career in medicine (Ward, 1986). A few other writers who initially practiced medicine include Oliver Wendell Holmes, Anton Chekhov, and Sir Arthur Conan Doyle, who wrote about Sherlock Holmes and Dr. Watson. Other physician/writers include Walker Percy, Somerset Maugham, Frank Slaughter, Michael Crichton, A. J. Cronin, and Robert Cook. John Locke left medicine and secured his place in history as a philosopher. Some have continued practicing medicine while pursuing successful additional careers on the side. Albert Schweitzer was a noted musician and philosopher. Benjamin Rush, a Philadelphia physician, worked tirelessly as a founding father of the United States and signed the Declaration of Independence. Dr. James McHenry, a physician for whom Fort McHenry was named, served as the secretary of war.

In his small book, *Call Me a Doctor,* Dr. Jack Griffitts describes six doctors who chose other pursuits (Griffitts, 1991). He discusses the life of Dr. James Long, Andrew Jackson's personal physician, who cared for the wounded at the battle of New Orleans and later became a fighting soldier himself. While battling for Texas, he met his death in Mexico. Dr. Griffitts also relates the story of Dr. James Wilkinson, who served as the governor of the Louisiana Territory. Dr. Wilkinson accused Aaron Burr of dirty dealings with Mexico and brought this now-historical issue to the forefront. Dr. William Walker led incursions into Nicaragua and helped establish a democratic government there. Still another doctor, Leander Starr Jameson, switched careers and led Jameson's Raiders into Rhodesia. The famous Dr. Leonard Wood became an army general who influenced President Theodore Roosevelt and encouraged him to form the Rough Riders. (Many of us know Dr. Wood as a patient of Dr. Harvey Cushing, who removed a recurrent meningioma several times from Dr. Wood's cranial cavity.) Finally, Dr. Frederick Cook left medicine to become an explorer. He is credited as one of the earliest explorers of the North Pole and some regard him as the North Pole's discoverer. Whether or not he was actually there is still debated.

Dr. Alister MacKenzie left his medical practice in England to become a golf course architect (Pasov, 1992). Although he was not a very good golfer, he designed courses that would allow poor golfers to have fun *and* would be ideal for tournament play. Examples of his courses include Cypress Point, Royal Melbourne, and the Augusta National Golf Course, which he worked on with Bobby Jones. MacKenzie observed that "the ideal golf architect should have made a study, from a golfing point of view, of agriculture, chemistry, botany, and geology." Furthermore, he felt that the study of psychology was "of great service in estimating what is likely to give the greatest pleasure to the greatest number."

In addition to the historical examples cited above, many contemporary physicians have left the bedside. Of the approximately 550,000 physicians in the United States, an estimated 100,000 serve in nonclinical positions. While doctors in administrative and management positions have changed their careers, these careers have evolved naturally, much as a corporate employee eventually becomes a manager, administrator, or chairman of the board.

In October 1991, Dr. Richard Wilke published a study in *Medical Care* titled "Practice Mobility among Young Physicians" (Wilke, 1991). He found a 10 percent chance that physicians will change practices within three years after they finish training and approximately a 33 percent chance of their changing practices within the first five years, and that doctors who start out self-employed are less likely to change their practices than those who work for Health Maintenance Organizations. He feels that doctors might join an HMO with limited information available to them initially, only to regret their decision later, but adds that the HMO experience can be useful for acquiring knowledge about practice arrangements.

While most physicians who modify their careers enter some phase of medical management, some choose other paths. Examples include employment in a radiology laboratory, working with disabled physicians, reviewing malpractice cases, processing claims for peer review organizations, estate planning, evaluating medical practices for buyouts, creating computer applications for medicine, medical publishing, preparing witnesses for malpractice trials, inventing, fundraising for various organizations, and corporate employment. Doctors have become authors or technical writers in varied fields. Some have joined their spouses in business ventures. Others have become involved in alternative health delivery systems, such as home health care or home infusion service. Without having received much additional training, some doctors are now involved with utilization review or quality assurance jobs for hospitals, insurance companies, or the government. Some have returned to medical schools as professors or teach alcoholics and drug users. Other physicians perform physical exams for the airline industry or fill in for doctors with a *locum tenens* assignment. Some have returned to school to earn degrees in law, business, or other specialties. Doctors commonly work with pharmaceutical companies in all phases of their work, including the preclinical or discovery phase, the clinical trials, patient testing, or even the selling and monitoring of drugs.

The records are replete with physicians who have been successful entrepreneurs. Dr. Robert Becker founded HealthCare Compare, a utilization and management company in Downers Grove, Illinois. In 1987, this company posted revenues of $11.6 million and continues to grow.

When Dr. Leonard Berger graduated from the University of Maryland Medical School, he imagined that he would spend the rest of his career as a medical doctor. He served a straight medical internship and did a year as a junior assistant resident in medicine at Saint Agnes Hospital. While in medical school he had been in the army reserves and was attached to the Ninety-second Field Hospital at Walter Reed Army Hospital. His unit was activated during the Berlin crisis and he was sent to Fort Gordon, Georgia. Later, in 1962, he entered private practice with a partner just outside of Baltimore and enjoyed practicing medicine and teaching at the university for a number of years.

Six years later he became interested in the nursing home business, bought first one and later two additional homes, and eventually sold all three to a partnership. In addition, he purchased the Perring Racquet Club and expanded it to the Perring Athletic Club. He bought apartments as well as more nursing homes in Laurel and Wheaton, Maryland, and in Ohio. Later on, he was able to sell all of the nursing homes.

In 1978, he became less enchanted with the growing regulation of medicine and he could foresee the future demise of private medical practices. He began to limit his practice to three days a week and purchased a cable franchise, becoming the president of Calvert Communications. He then began building a cable system, was able to get more financing, and had 1,700 stockholders. In 1983, he sold the company to Comcast, but stayed on as the chairman of the Baltimore Comcast System. He retired completely from his medical practice in 1983, in part because of a bout of pericarditis.

He then became involved with automobile dealerships. In 1985, he bought the Sheraton Hotel in Ocean City and added considerable space for a convention center. Since then, he has acquired several more automobile dealerships.

Dr. Berger advises physicians who wish to leave their medical practice and enter the business world to get some business training. He would discourage physicians from going into a business with friends who say they know the business, particularly if the doctors don't know the business themselves. He adds that times are not as propitious now as they were years ago to borrow money for a start-up business. He warns against giving any money up front to a firm or a person seeking to acquire start-up capital financing. He suggests that several physicians pool their finances, hire the right person, and then start their own business venture. He thinks it is much safer and easier to buy common stock in well-recognized companies than it is to manage a company from the beginning.

Dr. Theodore King finished his doctoral work in physiology and biochemistry in addition to his residency in obstetrics-gynecology at Johns Hopkins Hospital. He continued to do research at the Rockefeller Institute and served as professor of obstetrics and gynecology at Albany, New York, in 1968 and at Johns Hopkins Hospital from 1971 to 1991. Later on, he went to work as an executive for the Family Health International, doing research in the field of fertility management.

Dr. King became active in hospital management in 1983 and served as vice president of Medical Affairs at Johns Hopkins Hospital. Throughout his career, he has focused on fertility management and elective abortion. Although his venue has changed and he is with a nonprofit organization, he thinks he is doing what he has always done, primarily mixing research with medical management. Dr. King feels that doctors acquire certain skills during their years of training that prepare them for various opportunities; these skills include listening, empathizing, investigating, and managing. He doesn't feel that physicians really change careers when they stop seeing patients, but that they transfer laterally to some other endeavor that is somehow related.

Dr. Philip Wagley completed his residency training at Johns Hopkins Hospital and began practicing internal medicine. In the early 1970s, he became concerned with numerous ethical questions facing medicine. After researching the subject and writing about the issues, he was asked to teach medical ethics to the students at Johns Hopkins Medical School. His interest in ethics led him to the Kennedy Center in Washington, D.C., and also to the Hastings Institute. Although he continued to practice medicine until 1990, he is presently on the board of directors of the Hastings Institute and primarily deals with ethical issues such as euthanasia, assisted death, and the hospice movement. He has studied the idea of patients' autonomy, how much society should spend to keep patients alive, and the conflict between patients' demands and physicians' thoughts about a meaningful life. He has tackled such issues as what the actual goals of medicine are, how we can apportion the available revenues to the practice of medicine, and whether everyone who wants a heart transplant and qualifies for the procedure should get one. He has also been concerned with the growth of knowledge about genetics. There are issues about how much to tell patients and insurance companies about patients' genetic makeup and predisposition.

In addition to his interest in ethics, Dr. Wagley has a keen interest in the preservation of birds, is an avid ornithologist, and has been active with the Wild Fowl Trust of North America. Currently, he is the president of this organization.

Congressman Jim McDermott finished medical school at the University of Illinois in Chicago in 1963. He then did his residency in psychiatry. He fulfilled his military obligation as a psychiatrist in Long Beach, California, and began his practice soon afterward in Seattle, Washington. In 1970, he was elected to the Washington state legislature. He won a seat on the state senate in 1974 and was reelected in 1978,

1982, and 1986. In the meantime, he ran unsuccessfully for governor in 1972, 1980, and 1984. A few years after his last gubernatorial defeat, he left his job as state senator and decided to go into medicine full-time. He worked for the State Department as a medical officer and was sent to Zaire in this capacity. In 1988, Dr. McDermott ran successfully for the United States Congress. He then quit medicine and became a full-time congressional representative for Washington state. He has written Bill HR1200, which is titled The American Security Health Act. This is a single-payer system similar to that in Canada and Germany. It is a federally financed benefit package in which the health care system is run through an administration at the state level. Patients can choose their own provider. Most of the insurance companies will have a minimal role.

Representative McDermott states that he has really had two careers that he loved and he tried to do both of them for many years. Only when he became a member of Congress did he have to give up medicine completely and devote all of his energies to his political duties. He regards this as a natural evolution. He did not have any specific revelation in which he decided to leave medicine, but rather was attracted to both careers at an early stage in his life. His metamorphosis proceeded naturally from there.

After a successful career in neurosurgery, Dr. Clark Watts is changing professions. Having already earned master's degrees in pharmacology and public health, Dr. Watts served at the University of Missouri as chairman of the Department of Neurosurgery and was one of the first editors of *Neurosurgery*. Dr. Watts retained his commission in the U.S. Army Reserve and was pivotal at the Pentagon during the Desert Storm campaign in Kuwait. He recently finished law school and plans to establish a career in that field. Dr. Watts feels that doctors should plan early for life after neurosurgery and thinks it is just as important to prepare, train, and plan for a career in the later years as it was to study and prepare to be a neurosurgeon.

On November 3, 1992, Dr. Howard Dean was elected governor of Vermont. Dr. Dean graduated from Yale University in 1971 and received his medical degree in 1978 from Albert Einstein College of Medicine. In 1981, he began to practice medicine in Shelburne, Vermont. One year later, he was elected to the Vermont House of Representatives. In 1986, he was elected lieutenant governor and was reelected in 1988. Presently, he serves as cochairman of the National Governors' Association Health Care Task Force. Hillary Rodham Clinton named him to President Clinton's Health Care Task Force.

Dr. Richard Berczeller practiced medicine in Austria until 1938, when the Gestapo arrested him for being Jewish. He was released on the condition that he leave the German Reich. He stayed in Paris for a while supporting himself as a physician in a brothel before securing work as a medical assistant on the Ivory Coast. In 1941, he arrived in New York, where he studied and passed his medical examinations, which enabled him to practice medicine on the Lower East Side and on the staff of the Beth Israel Hospital. In his later life, he became a short-story writer and published numerous short stories and two books, one of which was *Displaced Doctor*.

In Annapolis, Maryland, in the 1950s, a black doctor named Aris Allen had difficulty obtaining privileges at the Anne Arundel Hospital because of racial discrimination. As the times changed so did this situation, and he later became chief of staff. Dr. Allen was elected and reelected to the Maryland House of Representatives for many years. During the Reagan presidency, he presided over one of the Republican national conventions.

Dr. Torrey Brown of Annapolis, Maryland, had planned to become a physician since early childhood. His parents strongly encouraged him to prepare for this discipline. He graduated from Wheaton College and went to Johns Hopkins University for his medical education and postgraduate training, which consisted of a one-year internship and three years of residency in internal medicine. He stayed at Johns Hopkins, planning a career in academic medicine and serving as chief of Emergency Medical Services from 1966 to 1971 and as director of Personnel Health Services from 1971 to 1978, following which he was selected as director of Outpatient Services from 1978 to 1983. While carrying out these duties, he was elected in 1970 to the House of Delegates of the Maryland Legislature. He was reelected by his constituents in Baltimore City in 1974 and again in 1978 but because of redistricting did not win reelection in 1982. While Dr. Brown served as the assistant dean of clinical programs at Johns Hopkins, Governor Hughes appointed him secretary of the Maryland Department of Natural Resources in 1983. Governor Schaefer reappointed him to this position in 1986 and 1990. His responsibilities in this role include overseeing the operation of a state agency with a staff of 1,630 people and an annual budget of $160 million. The Department of Natural Resources is responsible for protecting, conserving, and determining the best use for Maryland's natural resources. The department must develop policy, set legislative agendas, and implement these programs.

Besides these major jobs, Dr. Brown has been appointed associate professor of medicine at Johns Hopkins, chairman of the Board of Trustees, vice chairman of the Board of Directors of the Baltimore Zoological Society, and medical consultant to the National Basketball Association. He is a member of the Scenic and Wild River Review

Board, the Emergency Management Advisory Council, the Susquehanna River Basin Commission, the State Soil Conservation Committee, the Chesapeake Bay Critical Area Commission, the Governor's Council on the Chesapeake Bay, the Board of Trustees of the Chesapeake Bay Trust, the Committee on Alcoholism and Chemical Dependency of the Medical and Chirurgical Faculty of Maryland, and the Governor's Commission on Growth in the Chesapeake Bay Region. Dr. Brown also serves on the Hazardous Substance Research Center Advisory Council.

For the past three years, he has served as chief executive officer of Family Health International in Research Triangle Park, North Carolina. This organization is a nonprofit biomedical research and technical assistance organization dedicated to contraceptive development, family planning, reproductive health, and AIDS prevention around the world. His responsibilities include overseeing policy and planning, as well as implementing programs for Family Health International, which has 450 employees and an annual budget of $45 million.

Dr. Brown is very much concerned about the future of the health care delivery system in this country. He fears that it will become even more bureaucratic than it already is. He is also concerned about the professional liability problem, which he tried to reform by coauthoring a bill when he was a delegate in the Maryland state legislature.

Tom Langfitt always wanted to be a doctor. His father, a general surgeon in West Virginia, inspired him to follow in his footsteps. After graduating from Princeton, the younger Langfitt went to Johns Hopkins, where he acquired his medical education and later his neurosurgical training. Initially, he wanted to train in general surgery, but when he met Dr. Frank Otenasek and Dr. John Chambers, he decided he liked neurosurgery better. After his residency, he spent several years in the U.S. Army, where he was assigned a medical research position at Edgewood arsenal. Later, he spent a year in the laboratory of Dr. Earl Walker at Johns Hopkins. For a while afterward, he was able to practice neurosurgery and do research in neurophysiology. He left Baltimore to become the head of neurosurgery at the Pennsylvania Hospital and an associate in neurosurgery at the University of Pennsylvania. In 1968, he became the Charles Harrison Frazier Professor and director of the Division of Neurosurgery at the Hospital of the University of Pennsylvania. He became vice president of Health Affairs in 1973. While he was working in neurosurgery, he also served on the Board of Directors of Glenmeade Trust Company. In 1986, political turmoil erupted at the Glenmeade Trust and a search began for a new company president. During this time, Dr. Langfitt served as the acting president. In 1987, the board asked him to serve as the full-time chairman of the board, CEO, and president of Glenmeade.

Dr. Langfitt does not miss clinical medicine. He has stayed active in the health care arena and has continued to be involved in neuroscience research. He would advise doctors to be cautious about changing careers and to make such a change only after substantial exploration. He feels that the managed care trend is inexorable and that there will be a surplus of specialists in the near future. He expresses concern that most neurosurgeons may not have the talent or real interest that is required to change careers.

Dr. John Donovan helped establish the birth defects center at the Tufts New England Medical Center. Because he felt he could make a larger contribution to the medical world, he left the bedside and entered the world of electrical engineering. After writing a textbook in engineering, he helped establish a research organization in information systems at the MIT Sloan School of Management. Now he is president and chief executive of the Cambridge Technology Group, a three-year-old information systems training company in Cambridge, Massachusetts. He thinks he may leave the business world in a few years and enter public service.

Dr. Charles W. Hannah practiced obstetrics-gynecology from 1970 to 1984. He then stopped practicing obstetrics and did only gynecology until 1991. Because he was no longer deriving any satisfaction from his practice, he began attending Jones School of Law at Faulkner University, graduating in December 1992. Now he works as the medical director at the Southeast Alabama Medical Center and is the director of Risk Management. Dr. Hannah says that he was dissatisfied with his life as a doctor for several reasons; the loss of physician autonomy, the fear of malpractice suits, and the harassment from managed-care organizations and third-party insurance carriers all made him see the future of medicine as dismal. Now Dr. Hannah is very happy and feels enthusiastic about his career.

By far, most physicians who have modified their careers have entered the management field. Thus, the American College of Physician Executives has grown rapidly. But the number of physician executives barely keeps up with the escalating opportunities for those skilled in both administration and clinical medicine. The positions may be entitled department chief, physician administrator, medical director, vice president for Medical Affairs, or chief executive officer.

In her article in the *Southern Medical Journal,* "Physicians—Executives Past, Present and Future," Karen Smallwood observes that "a practicing doctor can become an executive by acquiring management training. This training can come from short courses in management or a master's degree in business administration or health care" (Small-wood and Wilson, 1992). She says there is no substitute for actual management experience. This is an important point, because some doctors fantasize that they could just leave their practice and become CEO of a large pharmaceutical or insurance company if they only had the right connections. Whether the field is law, business, or health care management, doctors should equate their skills in a new field with the skills that an intern in medicine possesses.

*Roads to Medical Management: Physician Executives' Career Decisions*, which Wesley Curry edited, describes contemporary physicians who have entered new management careers (Curry, 1988). Bernard Ferrari, who acquired M.D., J.D., and MBA degrees, states: "Physicians have to be able to take their place with legislators, lawyers, accountants, and the like, who are, in fact, deciding how physicians are going to practice medicine in the future" (Ferrari 1988). He adds: "I am still convinced, as I was during my residency at UCLA, that if physicians are to protect the profession, they must be represented by those physicians articulate in the language of other health care policy makers." Dr. Ferrari believes that because of the changes in the way medicine is regulated and the way doctors are paid, health care physician-executives will be instrumental in stabilizing a turbulent medical environment. Moreover, the changes represent opportunities and challenges for many physicians.

Some doctors wonder in amazement how their lives have changed. What started out as a logical, step-by-step pursuit of a medical career has turned to thoughts of career modification. External forces intrude upon life plans, catching people in a bind. They may feel out of control. Few expected that they would ever face such a change. They may feel too old. But it becomes necessary to change with the times. As one adapts one's perspective, inconvenience and fear of change will diminish. Change can propel us on to something better than what was left behind. Once doctors in transition stop resisting change, they can start thinking of themselves as a product. Then they need to learn the market and begin marketing themselves.

Markey and Parks in the *Monthly Labor Review* regard occupational mobility as helping the economy operate smoothly (Markey and Parks, 1989). This process allows workers to find more satisfying jobs. In *Second Careers: New Ways to Work After 50*, Caroline Bird points out that workers over fifty have a lower absenteeism rate and a better work ethic (Bird, 1992). In addition, they are more productive and stay with a job longer. Some switch occupations in order to accumulate marketable skills or increase their pay. Claudia Morain notes that the proportion of physicians in private office–based practice slipped to 58.7 percent in 1990 from 63.5 percent in 1965 (Morain, 1992).

Doctors should involve their entire family in any decision to change careers. It can be unsettling and uncomfortable for a spouse not to know exactly what plans are forthcoming. When doctors change careers, their children may feel anxious about being able to afford college. Doctors have to make the ultimate decision concerning their careers, but they should consider the financial and emotional effects on all the immediate family members, the loss of physician identity, and the possible diminution of self-esteem.

There are numerous nonclinical opportunities for physicians. In *Careers in Medicine: Traditional and Alternative Opportunities*, Rucker and Keller list over nine hundred possibilities (Rucker and Keller, 1986). When all is said and done, investigation, patience, and imagination can lead to a more enriching and rewarding career.

# Chapter 6

## "Managed Careers" in the Future

Consider a suburban scene that would have been unthinkable a few years ago. A highly trained urological surgeon is working in the yard at eleven in the morning. Displaced by the health care reform movement and managed care, he consorts with managers who have also lost their jobs as companies hurt by the recession have downsized, laying off skilled personnel. Most of these unemployed managers and doctors have converted bedrooms into makeshift offices while they search for full-time or part-time work. Some have volunteered for various positions at schools and churches, while many unemployed doctors go to support groups, many of which were started in hospitals.

These doctors frequent libraries looking for positions in the health care field. They skip social functions and tell former friends they are "consulting." Meanwhile, they exhaust their savings and take early distributions from pension plans that they built in earlier years.

Most of these doctors are in their early fifties and could not adjust to the new realities of the health care reform movement. Refusing to give up their autonomy, they will not join organizations that bid for patients on a capitated basis (meaning a flat fee for each person covered by the health plan). These unemployed doctors would rather swing a golf club in their backyard than consider primary-care retraining or reentering the work force in a less rewarding and prestigious capacity.

Dr. Marciana Wilkerson is an obstetrician in solo practice in Washington, D.C. She had been involved with a managed-care delivery system for a number of years. Without warning her or giving her any appeal mechanism, the HMO in which she participated arbitrarily dropped her and reduced her patient load by 20 percent (Goldstein, 1994).

She was the second black, female obstetrician-gynecologist to start practicing in the District of Columbia and she has built a good practice, delivering around 175 babies per year. She is very active in medical community affairs, serving as the medical director of Planned Parenthood of Metropolitan Washington, as a board member of Healthy Babies, a coalition that tries to curb infant mortality, and as a member of the Health Plus HMO Peer Review Committee.

Because she has been so irritated by the restrictions of the various managed-care plans, the arbitrary deselectiveness of the HMOs, and the possibility of even more "managed care" for everyone, she has been considering switching her career to home decorating, something she did to work her way through college and medical school.

In a recent survey by Foster Higgins, 102 organizations who give their employees the choice of joining managed-care plans ranked various factors in their choice of health care organizations. Sixty-nine percent of the companies ranked price as the most important factor and 9 percent ranked outcomes research statistics as important (Winslow, 1994a). Presently, price is what makes companies push their employees into managed-care groups. Many doctors think that as time goes by, prices will become more uniform and will matter less. Then, the quality of care and outcomes research statistics will propel one group of providers ahead of others.

Presently, HMOs are enjoying record profits. Most are seeing 20 percent annual growth in profits and some have increased their profits by as much as 73 percent in one year (Winslow, 1994b). In fact, HMOs take a central role in the Clinton health plan proposal. Currently, HMOs' profits come from growing enrollments, but later will depend on doctors' and hospitals' co-operation and skillful management. Oxford Health Plans, Inc., reported a 73 percent jump in earnings for the fourth quarter of 1993, while U.S. Healthcare posted a 33 percent earnings increase. Employers' attitudes about "cost consciousness," the managed-care "culture" of cost containment, the HMOs' desire for increased earnings, increased shareholder value, and increased stock prices are exacting a high price from patients and doctor-employees alike. Total quality management may seem ideal in the abstract, but this concept has no place in American medicine or in real people's lives.

The managed-care system depends heavily on a low doctor-patient ratio. Reportedly, Kaiser employs 1.3 doctors for every thousand patients, a ratio lower than the national HMO average (Salerno, 1994). Still, doctors weigh the benefits and the costs of any treatment, keeping in mind that, within the capitation agreement, doctors assume the risk insurance companies used to take.

Rationing care is part of the managed-care culture, requiring doctors to get approval for most tests and forms of therapy. They are more likely to base their decisions on budgetary limits than on a patient's health needs. In December 1992, Kaiser reported in their own magazine that two-thirds of their members were dissatisfied and that they lost 62,700 subscribers in one year.

Dr. Edward Rankin of Washington has become increasingly disenchanted with "managed care." For example, a patient of his had pain in her hand so severe that it awakened her in the night. Only by shaking her hand could she get any relief or any sleep. Her thumb and index finger were numb and she had a positive Tinel's sign. In addition, she had a positive peripheral nerve conduction test that indicated a carpal tunnel syndrome. Dr. Rankin tried to schedule a decompression of the median nerve, only to be told by the HMO that a case reviewer had denied permission for surgery, suggesting instead that the patient use hand splints for two months (Goldstein, 1994). Only after Dr. Rankin spent several hours on the phone talking to an orthopedic case reviewer did the HMO agree to the proposed surgery. Dr. Rankin is concerned that health care reform will create even more bureaucracy, and more obstacles to good health care, with the ultimate erosion of the system to which we have become accustomed. He wonders whether some other occupational endeavor would be more worthwhile.

As the health care debate intensifies, doctors are worried about their professional future and are examining the various possibilities. Few experts believe that the proposed Clinton plan will emerge intact through the legislative process. Even if there are significant modifications in the original proposal, the future most likely will emphasize the use of HMOs and "easier access" to health care for all Americans. Here, "easier access" is a code word and euphemism for gatekeeper physicians and mandatory participation in HMOs. Many criticize the Clinton plan for its vague ideas about paying for what it has proposed. Few believe that controlling the cost of health care can generate enough savings to extend coverage to the uninsured.

Suzanne Tregarthen writes in the *Wall Street Journal* that health care costs are overstated (Tregarthen, 1993). She says that the medical price index, computed by the Bureau of Labor Statistics, uses "list prices," which bear little resemblance to the actual "transaction" price. Even though hospitals and doctors charge "list" prices, most providers participate with plans that pay discounted "transaction" prices.

A second distortion relates to the effect quality has on cost. The hospital consumer price index uses per-day hospital charges. Many surgical procedures have improved so much that they can now be done as outpatient procedures, which automatically alters the reported health care statistics. A health care "crisis" may not be as ominous as some would lead us to believe.

Specialist physicians do have several choices and should be aware of them. First, they can lobby and work for a health care system that gives the patient more power, as advocated by John C. Goodman and Gerald Musgrave in their book, *Patient Power* (Goodman and Musgrave, 1992). Second, specialists can join physician hospital organizations (PHOs). Third, specialists can form multispecialty groups or clinics. Finally, specialists can do none of the above and take their chances that they will remain happily employed.

Goodman and Musgrave discuss an agenda for change in which individuals can buy catastrophic insurance at a reasonable price. They feel that individuals should have a chance to choose among the various competing health plans, especially between the employer plan with income tax benefits and the family plan, which should not have income tax penalties. They state that individuals should be able to choose between self-insurance and third-party insurance for small medical bills. Individuals could build their own reserve by saving for future medical expenses and then compare prices in the hospital marketplace.

They propose the following measures: establishing equity and taxing health insurance; equalizing tax advantages for families with unequal income; disposing of tax subsidies for wasteful health insurance; creating individual self-insurance for small medical bills; creating freedom of choice in health insurance and freedom of information in the hospital marketplace; encouraging people to save for postretirement medical expenses; creating catastrophic health insurance coverage for the elderly; avoiding the costs of the tort system; creating medical enterprise zones; and employing a cost-benefit standard for health and safety regulatory agencies (Goodman and Musgrave, 1992).

Their goals for an ideal health care system would be to: transfer power from large institutions and bureaucracies to individuals; restore the buyer/seller relationship to patients and medical suppliers so that the patients rather than third-party insurers become the principal buyers of health care; create institutions in which patients spend their own money rather than someone else's when they purchase health care; remove health care from the political arena in which well-organized special interests can cause great harm; subject the health care sector to the rigors of competition; and create market-based institutions in which individuals reap the full benefits of their good decisions and bear the full cost of their bad ones (Goodman and Musgrave, 1992).

Because of the intensity of health care reform, a growing interest has developed in integrating hospitals with medical groups. This phenomenon, which is happening all over the country, results from several key trends:(1) managed care is becoming the dominant form of health care delivery; (2) managed care itself is in transition; (3) the health care reform is already occurring; and (4) health care providers have assumed the risk that insurance companies once bore (Goodman and Musgrave, 1992).

Physicians and hospitals are joining forces to form

Physician Hospital Organizations (PHOs). These organizations would assess the risk, negotiate contracts, provide data, manage risks, and support physician practices. A PHO should strive to balance physicians' interests and hospitals' interests with the realities of the marketplace. It must address physician "control" issues and hospital issues. Finally, a PHO must support its objectives and functions.

Physicians are usually concerned with assuming risk. They want to have control over medical issues and influence over doctors who participate. They want to reduce the administrative hassle and paperwork, but they want utilization compliance. Laboring under the constraints of start-up costs, physicians have good reason to be concerned about the balance of power between the hospital and the doctors.

The hospital has to educate physicians about the changing environment. It must create an organized group of high-quality doctors and have the ability to deal with multiple groups of physicians. The hospital wants to accomplish medical staff development goals.

The PHO does differ from a more highly integrated alliance, such as a group practice without walls. The PHO is owned and governed either by the hospital or by the hospital and the physicians. The group practice without walls is wholly owned by physician shareholders. The PHO will be for profit or not-for-profit, taxable or tax exempt, whereas the group practice without walls is a for-profit professional medical corporation or medical partnership. PHO is the lowest degree of hospital/physician integration. The group practice without walls may not be as attractive to managed care in a competitive environment. The start-up cost for a PHO ranges from $50,000 to $150,000, and operating expenses run from $200,000 to $300,000 annually. The start-up cost for a group practice without walls runs about $30,000 to $60,000, depending on its size. The operating expenses are about 50 percent of its revenues. The advantages of a PHO are that it is a vehicle with which to organize the medical staff and that it preserves physician autonomy. The group practice without walls bears a low risk in organizing physicians and can attract capital for various ventures.

Upon starting a PHO, the organization has to deal with such issues as: the focus of PHO activities, ownership, governance, and issues directly involving physician participation, such as utilization, cost, quality, coverage, and the credentialling process. The organization must consider various forms of physician income distribution, such as discounted fees or capitation. They must choose among several risk-sharing techniques, including the issue of withholds. Another issue is how much authority to give the organization over physicians and over contracts with accountable medical plans. The issue of exclusivity is very important and has the potential to fragment a PHO. The organization must draw up rules for making contractual arrangements with outside providers and with competing providers.

Some factors remain important regardless of which organization is created. An organization's ability to manage its own costs and to maintain demonstrable quality is vital to its success. Sufficient capitalization from the beginning is critical. Finally, the doctors must have confidence in the management team.

To achieve a more fully integrated model, it would be wise to consider various models. One model would be a professional corporation that participates in a fully integrated delivery system owned by a few physicians and employing salaried doctors. A second model would focus on physicians who are employees of a fully integrated delivery system, such as the Mayo Clinic or the Ochsner Clinic. A third model would be where a physician-owned group practice offered a full range of wholly owned or network services. Finally, member physicians could also own a multispecialty group practice with long-term contracts to management.

A multispecialty group practice would be able to provide more capital and management skills to an organization than individual physicians alone could provide. Primary-care physicians would benefit from a multispecialty clinic by seeing more patients and being able to treat them better. Doctors would organize so that they could assume risk-bearing contracts. An organization would ideally give the primary-care physicians clout that they ordinarily would not have in dealing with HMOs and hospitals.

Specialists would also be attracted to such a group, because it would allow them to protect and enlarge their referral base, thus compensating for a decrease in the number of patients they see. They would optimally be able to grow volume and differentiate their skills in the competitive market.

All physicians would be interested in a multispecialty clinic in order to reduce practice costs and develop alternative sources of income from outpatient services and ancillary services. Such an organization should give doctors a collegial environment, access to capital that they didn't have before, and access to managed-care experts.

Certain factors are absolutely critical to the success of a multispecialty organization. There has to be an adequate primary-care network and the ability to assume the risk for a large number of enrollees. The group must demonstrate effective utilization management as well as outcome results. There has to be a stable and dependable performance record.

Why must doctors concern themselves with all of these plans and organizations? Certain key statistics explain why physicians should consider all of these options. Already there are more than 500 HMOs with 40 million members. These have at least a 22 percent penetration in the 30 largest cities in the United States. There are more than 770 PPOs with an estimated 45 million members. This means that HMOs and PPOs together have approximately 85 million members. Almost all indemnity carriers are moving to some type of managed care. Employers will be restricting employees' choice of health care providers based on cost containment and outcomes research results, which are quality concerns.

In the past few years, the balance of power has clearly shifted from physicians to large insurance companies. Nearly 90 million Americans get their health care through a managed-care network, such as an HMO or PPO. Several years ago, many doctors participated with these plans either as a convenience for some of their patients who wished to continue getting their medical care from their own doctor, or out of curiosity about that area of health care delivery. Now many doctors depend on the managed-care system for the majority of their patients and for their livelihood. The problem is that managed-care networks promised doctors that by delivering medicine at a discount, they would soon have a large volume of patients. Unfortunately, this never happened.

In addition to their disappointment over the low volume of patients, the markedly discounted fees, and the increased regulations and rules backed by punitive measures and fines, many physicians are now receiving letters from HMOs and PPOs informing them that their services are no longer needed (Winslow and Felsenthal, 1993). The physicians are in fact being fired without any due process, any hearings, and in many instances without any reason given. HMOs tell doctors that they no longer are needed purely from an economic point of view. While a release from an HMO is not technically the same as being fired, it means that a doctor may have insufficient patients to maintain a practice.

Although many doctors are taking these managed-care insurers to court, HMOs maintain that they are trying to provide high-quality, low-cost care. They claim they are weeding out physicians who order too many tests, too many procedures, and recommend too much surgery. The HMOs say they want to link up only with those physicians who share their outlook on medicine. Many doctors argue that randomly dismissing physicians inappropriately interferes with the doctor-patient relationship. The insurance companies plead that they must use economic credentialling and strategic considerations to form a more restrictive group. They say they can only compete in the new medical environment by providing high-quality care at a discount.

Doctors have been frustrated in their efforts to nail the giant insurance companies for violating antitrust laws. By joining together and forming various organizations, doctors have tried to gain bargaining leverage with which they could discuss individual physicians' dismissals from HMOs and negotiate their fee structure. The antitrust regulations presently prohibit doctors from collectively bargaining and health insurers obviously do not want these laws relaxed (Felsenthal, 1994). Senator Orrin Hatch (R-Utah) and Representative Bill Archer (R-Texas) have introduced legislation that would ease the antitrust laws and broaden the conditions under which doctors unite and discuss these issues as a group. Currently, President Clinton's plan does not allow doctors to bargain in strength with any managed-care organization.

Already, fee-for-service arrangements have been reduced. For example, a doctor sees a patient, performs a service, submits a claim to a third-party insurance carrier, and eventually receives full payment from the insurance company or receives a partial payment and then bills the patient for the balance. Large business organizations, state governments, and county governments are making capitation arrangements between hospitals and groups of physicians. In this prepaid system, the organization or government pays a fixed amount of revenue to a medical provider unit, which will then provide a certain population with health care for an agreed upon length of time. The provider unit accepts the inherent risk, rather than the insurance company. The amount of money varies with the number of patients covered in this plan and the benefits agreed upon in advance. The less work the provider unit does, the more profits it will reap; the more services it provides, the less money it makes. Both Clinton's health plan and other insurance-reform plans envision hospitals as the center of the capitated network.

Another payment arrangement is the managed fee-for-service plan in which the insurance company returns a withheld sum of money to the physicians if they have used fewer resources than were allocated. This is a hybrid arrangement of the fee-for-service and the capitated prepaid model. More often than not, all of the physicians will be punished if the resources are overused; none of the withheld revenues will be distributed. It is possible for some specialists to receive withheld distributions and to make more money by working mainly within their own field.

Currently, numerous parts of the health care delivery system fuel inflation and increase costs. The tax system creates incentives for employers to compensate the employees with health care insurance rather than increased wages. Employers began to pay their workers' health care premiums when the Internal Revenue Service ruled that such payments were tax deductible business expenses that were nontaxable to the employee. Years ago, the National Labor Relations Board encouraged employers and employees to bargain about health insurance and benefits. Despite a wage freeze during World War II, the War Labor Board encouraged employers to increase health benefits instead of wages. Predictably, the result has been an abuse of the system with many employees overusing the facilities.

The unique American tort system ·encouraged providers to practice defensive medicine. Now, doctors order more tests and give more care to diminish the chances of a lawsuit. The government pays for health care for the elderly and the indigent and imposes price controls for this care, which causes providers to shift the costs to the rest of their patients.

It is well known that more governmental involvement will lead to more bureaucracy, waste, corruption, and inefficiency. Socialist countries all over the world are turning away from such failed techniques and arrangements. Many Americans, however, embrace a single-payer socialized medical system. President Clinton is proposing that the government take care of everyone, even though the costs of health care in this country appear to be increasing more slowly.

Bart Giamatti expressed his views of government bureaucracy and regulations in his book, *A Free and Ordered Space* (Giamatti, 1988). "We learn, therefore, that there is no true freedom without order; we learn that there are limits to our freedom, limits we learn to choose freely in order not to undermine what we seek. After all, if there were, on the one hand, no restraints at all, only anarchy of intellect and chaos of community would result. On the other hand, if all were restraint, and release of inquiry and thought were stifled, only a death of the spirit and a denial of any freedom could result. There must be an interplay of restraint and release, of order and freedom, in our individual lives and in our life together. Without such interplay within each of us, there can be no good life for any of us. If there is no striving for the good life for all of us, however, there cannot be a good life for any one of us."

Congress has several proposals for health care reform to consider. Senator Phil Gramm has a bill for "medical IRAs," as John Goodman and Gerald Musgrave discuss in *Patient Power* (Goodman and Musgrave, 1992).

Managed competition and managed care have been successful in some areas of the country for some groups of people, but have not been tried long enough to be enforced among the entire population. Because this country is so large and diverse, we need to try different approaches before imposing one on the country and hoping that we don't precipitate a disaster for all.

# Chapter 7
# Preparing for the Health Care Revolution

## Malpractice Reform

There can be no health care reform without malpractice reform. President Clinton, supported by the trial lawyers, has proposed two ways to reform the medical malpractice situation. One is to implement "the collateral source rule." While this is already in place in many states, it has not effectively reduced the cost of malpractice insurance or awards. This plan suggests that plaintiffs first seek payments from their own insurance policies. If this is insufficient, they should seek to dip into the doctor's malpractice insurance policy. President Clinton also wants to cap attorneys' fees at 33 percent of what they win for their clients in malpractice suits. This is already what most attorneys obtain, so it will not be much of a reform.

David McIntosh (1993) says that damage caps have been the only effective means of reducing malpractice awards. He cites Indiana as a perfect example; premiums in Indiana are $4,350 a year, compared to $73,000 in Florida. He says that patients in Indiana who are truly injured receive larger awards.

# Canadian Health Care System

As health care reform is being debated, some supporters of the single-payer system cite the Canadian system as the one for the United States to emulate. Pam Politer (1993) states that Canada's federal government is actually reducing the amount it spends on the health system, because their economy is suffering and they are mired in debt. At the very time we seek to emulate their system, Canada happens to be looking for a more effective, less costly way to deliver health care.

In 1984, the Canadian Health Act passed, requiring all provincial and territorial plans to meet five conditions: the plans must be universal, comprehensive, successful, publicly administered, and portable (the insurance can be carried from job to job). Provinces may set their own insurance regulations and benefits with regard to other issues.

In 1991, according to Gilles Fortrin (1993), Canada spent $2,045 per capita or 9.9 percent of its gross domestic product on health care, whereas the United States spent $2,868 per capita or 13.2 percent of its GDP on health care. Whereas the life expectancy rate in Canada is identical to that in the United States, the infant mortality rate is 25 percent lower than in the United States.

Three reasons given for the lower cost of Canada's health care system include lower administrative overhead, lower hospital costs, and lower physician fees (U.S. General Accounting Office, 1991). The lower administrative costs are attributed to the fact that there is no patient billing and less paperwork for physicians. Furthermore, there are no costs for evaluating insurance risk and for marketing between competing plans.

Critics of the Canadian health care system point to its

outdated equipment, its overcrowded facilities, and the elimination of hospital beds and services. Certain surgical procedures and diagnostic tests are available only at a limited number of locations and are therefore inaccessible to some, inconvenient for others. There are waiting lists for various forms of medical care, especially for elective surgery.

One Canadian neurosurgeon who recently left Canada to practice in the United States said, "Of the eleven people who qualified as neurosurgeons in Canada two years ago, ten have gone to the United States." The July 25, 1994, cover story of *Maclean's*, Canada's leading magazine, describes how hospitals have cut services and laid off personnel since politicians have cut the health care budget. The waiting lists for surgery are growing and research has been stifled.

Although many people think the Canadians love their national health care system, interviews with several Canadian physicians reveal problems. Dr. Steve B. is a general surgeon in Canada who feels satisfied with the fact that he gets paid something for every patient, even if the amount is lower than he feels he deserves. He knows that the waiting lists for health care have grown and he works in a system with aged equipment, which is a reflection of the underinvestment in health technology. He states that Canada does not allow her citizens the right to seek private health care to avoid the lines and lists, but also that it does not prohibit them from crossing the border to get their health care and surgery from outstanding health centers in the United States. Whereas he knows of no Canadian physicians who have switched careers, he says numerous physicians and nurses have left Canada to seek better working conditions in the United States. Dr. Richard W. agrees that most physicians in Canada feel that the efficiency and quality of the health care system have declined since the advent of the national health service.

## Health Care in the United Kingdom

Dr. Louis D. has been practicing medicine in Great Britain for almost twenty-five years. He readily admits that he would rather practice in a current setting and a more favorable environment. Most British hospitals are in a state of disrepair. He feels that his colleagues do less of everything, including work. The English people are less likely to have surgery of any kind and only a fraction will have coronary bypass surgery. They get far fewer diagnostic studies and the women have Pap smears only once every five years, following doctors' orders.

Dr. D. thinks more and more people are electing to have their own private insurance so they can get treated on their own terms. He has heard of no doctor who has switched careers, except for a neurosurgeon in Scotland who has become member of Parliament. He does know of numerous doctors who have left the United Kingdom to practice in the United States. Most of their slots have been filled by doctors from foreign countries who have immigrated to the United Kingdom. He finds it incomprehensible that while most of the world is abandoning their socialist medical schemes and national health services, the United States is gravitating toward more governmental control of medical care.

## German Health Care System

As we reflect on our own system and look at other systems, we must examine the German health care system, which has universal coverage and a fee-for-service arrangement. Patients have the right to choose a doctor. According to Catherine Jeakle-Hill (1993), 90 percent of patients belong to one of the 1,100 sickness funds. Despite efforts to contain medical costs in Germany, the country still has a lot of financial problems, including the cost of changing the former East Germany's health care system.

The average length of stay in a German hospital is 12.3 days, as compared to seven days in the United States (Weil, 1992). Germany is trying to combat the long hospital stays by instituting a diagnosis-related group system similar to that in the United States. The problem of long-term health care in Germany still needs to be solved.

According to Frederic Jones in *Physician Executive* (1993), the German health care system is supported in large part by a government-mandated system of financing to which both employers and employees contribute. The government exercises control over hospital expenditures. Sickness funds established by statute as not-for-profit organizations collect revenues and turn them over to provider units on a negotiated-fee schedule basis. Both types of doctors—hospital specialists and ambulatory physicians, or out-of-hospital specialists—and hospitals are included in this arrangement. All German citizens have access to the health care system and can freely choose their physicians. Most Germans feel that this government intervention in their health care is necessary to provide every citizen with access.

There are, however, some significant problems with their health care system. For one thing, there are too many doctors in Germany. Only 10 percent of the ambulatory physicians are able to enter practice their first year, leaving a large number of physicians unemployed, as many as

1,500 in Berlin. Germany uses the health care system to re-distribute income from the affluent and healthy to the sick and poor. Many companies are taking their employees out of the sickness funds and are starting their own insurance companies. Recent reforms instituted in January 1993 limit the number of physicians under the statutory insurance system, institute diagnosis-related group systems of payment, and budget the amount of revenue that goes to physicians and prescription drugs.

According to Wilfried Prewo in Hanover, Germany, the chief executive of the Chamber of Industry and Commerce, Germany is not a model for the United States, despite what President Clinton and Senator Jay Rockefeller would have us believe (Prewo, 1994). The United States and Germany have completely different situations in terms of crime-related injuries, malpractice claims, and long-term nursing care arrangements. The cost of Germany's plan has risen 23 percent over the past three years after accounting for inflation.

The German health care system has been on the verge of bankruptcy for twenty years. Since 1977, nine federal laws have passed to control medical costs, prices, and supplies. Currently, Germany even has quotas on how many doctors can practice.

The German plan does not put its people first. There is no encouragement to save for future medical care and to assume responsibility for one's own health through proper eating, exercising, and refraining from excessive drinking and smoking. Because there is no copayment, Germans overuse their health care system. Germany already has a single-payer system financed by the payroll tax. In large part due to the medical system, Germany has the most expensive labor in the world after Switzerland and has a higher unemployment rate than the United States.

*   *   *

Unquestionably, medical practice as we have known it is rapidly disappearing. Whether we as practitioners have to deal with the vagaries of managed care or with the regulations of a single-payer system, we will have to adapt. Regardless of which system prevails, there will continue to be sick patients for doctors to treat and technological progress in medicine will move onward, despite all efforts to contain it.

Technology has already revolutionized the way we practice medicine. The information explosion in the field of genetics allows doctors to manufacture growth hormone from E. coli bacteria and to use this hormone to help children whose growth has been stunted. It is predicted that genetics will help treat neurosurgical problems, such as cancer and strokes, as well as spinal cord injuries. We are now treating brain abscesses with stereotactic surgery and powerful antibiotics. More brain tumors are being biopsied with stereotactic devices and then treated with concentrated radiation to a localized tumor. Many cerebrovascular problems are now being treated with endovascular embolization and coils.

Some questions remain unanswered. Who will be given medical treatment? Where will the treatment be provided? How will this treatment be financed. Across the country, the health care industry is consolidating. Peter Bent Brigham and Women's Hospital in Boston is merging with the Massachusetts General Hospital in an effort to survive the health care reform movement. Many other hospitals are trying to cut their expenses by reducing the number of hospital beds, laying off personnel, and instituting a hiring freeze.

If hospital and hospital supply company contraction continues, we may come to feel that there are too many specialists in the United States. Surgical specialists might have to move to major metropolitan hospitals to continue performing complicated surgical procedures. Some surgical specialists may have to become gatekeepers for their specialty, letting other doctors in that specialty perform the surgical procedures, not unlike the German system of hospital doctors and nonhospital doctors who evaluate, diagnose, prepare people for surgery, and help take care of them afterward.

Some physicians, particularly the younger ones, will be able to adapt to the changes with little difficulty. They will have never experienced medicine any other way and will fit right into a system that remunerates them at a lower scale, probably with some risk-bearing capitation method. Older doctors will also have to adapt or will have to retire earlier than planned or direct their energies to some other field.

Not all doctors will actually embrace one alternative or the other. Some will continue practicing medicine on a reduced scale, maintaining their autonomy, self-respect, and identity as surgical specialists They might also get involved in some other field. Some doctors may continue to see patients and practice medicine with a group. They might also continue practicing on a fee-for-service basis and work in medical management as a hired employee of some group.

# Chapter 8

# Business Ventures

For some doctors who are unhappy with the current state of American medicine, business ventures may seem appealing. There are numerous ways to become involved with business, but one of the safest is by purchasing stock in companies. This technique provides a great deal of liquidity as long as the companies are public, not closely held or thinly traded. This arrangement frees doctors from the day-to-day management of any particular business. They can end their involvement very quickly if they are unhappy with a company's goals and results. Such an arrangement can be profitable and enjoyable to those who like to follow business endeavors, trends, and industries. Doctors who pursue this path must discipline themselves to stay with their stocks and companies as the markets fluctuate. Over the long term, however, investing in the stock market may be just the right avenue for those who don't want the risks involved in owning and managing a business.

Starting a company can be difficult during these times of restricted lending practices, especially after the savings and loan debacle. Obtaining loans from family members may work better than trying to borrow from unscrupulous lenders who demand up-front money and charge high interest rates. Some advisers urge entrepreneurs not to start a business without adequate capitalization and fallback resources for any additional financing that will be needed. There is a high failure rate with start-up companies, which can be discouraging. Starting one's own company brings up some important questions. Besides facing issues of financing, the new entrepreneur must know the competition and the market. Mr. Ken Heller of Denver, Colorado, started a company ten years ago named NuTech Environmental Corporation. His company makes auto-controlled technologies and it took him a while to understand the market. He feels he wasted two years cold-calling potential customers until he figured out which industries had a definite use for his product.

Franchises are worth examining as a potential business. They provide a certain amount of comfort, but at a loss of money and freedom. When I decided to enter a business venture, my first idea was to buy a franchise that helps students with their education. I researched this project and went to the franchiser's corporate headquarters with a prospective partner. I finally decided against this venture because the franchisers wanted the owner to be actively involved in teaching at the franchise.

My next idea was to start a business using CD-ROM technology which might have been successful had so many people not been entering this new field. I also considered buying a franchise in the postal preparation companies, such as Mailboxes Etc. This really didn't suit me because there was no barrier to entry. Finally, my difficulties in getting good secretarial help, particularly with regard to medical transcription, gave me the idea of trying to revolutionize the transcription industry.

When I founded Transcriptions International, I realized that I could not serve two masters at the same time. Because actively practicing neurosurgery was my first priority, and because I did not plan to leave neurosurgery until I was satisfied with every aspect of my start-up business, I decided to run Transcriptions International with a delegating style of management. Unfortunately, this made the company's future hinge on the people I hired. Regardless of how much money you invest in any business, the business's success depends on the personnel involved. Even though it is extremely important to make excellent personnel choices from the start, and I cannot stress this enough, it is very difficult to be certain about people until you have worked with them. If you think your patients can be litigious, wait until you start dealing with employees in a business. They can sue you for everything from the terms of the employment and the benefits to a so-called "wrongful discharge." To avoid such problems, it is best to set the business's policies right away with regard to salary, salary increases, sick days, holidays, overtime, and job responsibilities.

Just as Mr. Ken Heller had difficulty identifying his customers, so did we at Transcriptions International. Initially, my plan was to approach the medical transcription business from a computer point of view and to develop software that would enable us to obtain medical dictation from hospitals, clinics, and doctors' offices anywhere in the United States. The goal was to have all of this oral dictation gathered in Annapolis. Then, transcriptionists in the United States and in foreign countries could access the dictation, type it up, and send it back to Annapolis. Computers would make it possible to transcend geographic limits. While this would incur some satellite transmission costs, we could take advantage of the lower labor costs in other parts of the country and world. Although I was able to get the company up and running and eventually sold it to others, I want to share some of the problems I encountered so that others can anticipate and avoid such pitfalls.

There was certainly a need for Transcriptions International. It has become more difficult for doctors to find competent medical transcriptionists. Our inadequate public educational system does not produce high school graduates who can spell, use correct grammar, have word-processing computer skills, and know medical terminology. This is even truer in rural areas and smaller towns. Having experienced difficulty obtaining excellent transcription work in my own office, I felt that other doctors must desperately need this service. Transcriptions International gave doctors anywhere the ability to pick up the telephone, dial an 800 number to our computer, dictate as long as they want, and have the dictation returned to them on their own computer within twenty-four hours. The doctor's staff could make any corrections or changes right there on the spot, without sending the dictation back to the transcriptionist. The problem we encountered was that this service required that we adapt our software to each doctor's computer. We were surprised to learn that there were so many different computer arrangements. We would have to send a computer expert to each doctor's office to set up the doctor's computer and train the office staff, a task that varied depending on the level of computer literacy and sophistication in each doctor's office. All this adaptation, training, and travel added to the overhead expenses, lowered the profit level, and created frustration and conflict, which the venture had aimed to reduce in the first place.

Our second major problem involved timing. No one knew that the summer of 1990 would be the beginning of a severe recession. Because of massive job layoffs, the savings and loan debacle, and general economic uncertainty, neither hospitals nor doctors wanted to make any changes, even if we showed them where they could save money.

They postponed or decided against altering their transcription arrangements, which was discouraging to a start-up business. Because we really did not appreciate that hospitals and larger clinics would be our bigger customers, we probably wasted a lot of resources on telemarketing and direct-mail solicitations.

Interviewing, hiring, and training some transcriptionists brought more problems, some of which were humorous. Once we were going to interview someone to oversee the quality control of the transcriptionists and the actual transcriptions. The prospective applicant told me over the phone that she would be arriving at 5:00 P.M. on the flight from San Francisco. She said to look for a blond who was slightly overweight and carrying a yellow umbrella. She requested that I, too, have a yellow umbrella. As I waited for her to get off the plane, it seemed that all the women on that flight were blond and that several had yellow umbrellas—only one weighed 340 pounds and would not fit in the front seat of my car.

I eventually hired a different transcriptionist and sent her to the Caribbean to train additional transcriptionists. Unfortunately, the educational background of the new transcriptionists was simply not adequate for the job, even though their mastery of English was advertised as good. For example, a sentence dictated as "I saw the patient one day ago" would come back as "I saw the patient one diego."

I interviewed a very successful businessman from India and thought for a while that I would work with him on this project. We were able to solve the satellite transmission problems so that work dictated during the day in the United States would arrive in India during the night and could be typed when the workers appeared in the morning. They would then transmit their typing back to the United States, where it would be printed in the morning at hospitals, clinics, or doctors' offices. The major stumbling block was the labor relations arrangement in India: an employer who hires someone even for training is obliged to employ that person for life. My Indian counterpart was reluctant to hire someone who might not understand American accents and medical terminology, but was interested in exploring this further later on. I also talked with people in South Africa who were willing to come aboard, even though we had trouble arriving at an agreeable pay arrangement.

We also ran into problems with some government contracts. Not only do they pay badly, but many of them also stipulate that if the transcription work does not meet their standards and they therefore terminate their contract with your transcription company, they will bill you for any expense they incur obtaining transcription from another company for the duration of the contract. Signing this arrangement will obligate you to pay someone else for their transcription work without any definitive basis being agreed upon in advance.

A never-ending problem with most business enterprises is the constant need for capital. Start-up companies need money to pay all the bills and salaries until they have acquired equipment and a constant flow of cash. Transcriptions International was no exception and attempted to sell stock to pay back debts and to have a broader base of support for the company to expand. Unfortunately, this did not work out.

Most people want to invest in companies with a track record of enhancing value. As a start-up, it is very difficult to attract investors. Although thousands of small companies write well-conceived business plans and try to sell stock, only a minority succeed. The company has to be a solid investment with financial records that honestly depict growth and show that there is a growing market for the product and services. If it does go public, a company should have a comprehensive business plan, a competent management team, and sufficient capital for legal fees, accounting fees, and travel expenses to promote the investment. Companies that go public should be aware that every decision and transaction becomes open to public scrutiny. The company completely loses its privacy. A public company has to enhance shareholder value, show a profit, and be prepared to make changes in personnel and policy to achieve those goals.

The worst problem I had with the transcription company came from our own tax laws. I was told that since I owned 100 percent of my neurosurgical professional corporation and more than 85 percent of Transcriptions International, I would have to provide the same pension plan benefits for the people in Transcriptions International as for the personnel at the neurosurgical office. Because I was using contract laborers and because I employed many more personnel at Transcriptions International, this would not be economically feasible. I was also informed that the IRS was contesting the definition of contract labor and that they might very well insist that I withhold tax and pay FICA for all my contract laborers. This would eliminate our competitive advantage, especially because the Internal Revenue might very well hold me personally liable for back FICA and taxes, even though Transcriptions International was a Subchapter S corporation. Because I could not overcome these tax problems, I sold Transcriptions International to someone who would not face the same obstacles.

Any physician thinking of leaving medicine for business should be encouraged by the success story of Mrs. Field's Cookies. Mrs. Field started this successful business when she was twenty years old, uneducated, and penniless. Besides her cookie recipe, she had a determination to succeed where so many have failed. With perseverance, she obtained financing from a banker. She has expanded her business to over eight hundred stores, with some franchises abroad, and has grossed millions of dollars. Surely, if she could parlay a cookie recipe into such an enterprise when she lacked education, experience, and sufficient funds, a doctor who has all those things could create wealth in a business venture or in some investment arrangement.

Another alternative would be to purchase a successful enterprise and keep the management personnel. Experts estimate that most business buyers spend at least a year searching for an established business. A potential buyer may talk to ten or twenty owners before finding a suitable business. The expense of due diligence could run as high as twenty thousand dollars, including the costs of travel, legal advice, accounting services, and research, but this expenditure may be worthwhile. Questions to ask include: (1) Why is the owner selling the business? (2) Do I have the experience to run this business? (3) How does the company do against the competition? (4) Can the business pay an adequate salary and give a fair return on the investment? (5) Will my family support this venture? (6) Will the seller stay on or leave? (7) Do I have a good appraisal and good accounting advice?

Doctors can find someone to help them determine a fair purchase price. Then they will be able to study the business's track record and its competition. After buying the business, doctors will still lack liquidity, however, and will have to assume a risk, one that older doctors might not want to undertake at this stage in their life.

Some doctors may want to follow yet another path: using their experience to guide other players in the health industry. Having practiced medicine for a number of years, doctors are valuable as consultants to insurance companies, pharmaceutical companies, nursing home chains, and surgical supply companies. Health care consultants have really come into their own during this reform movement. Many are already selling their knowledge by encouraging doctors to form one of many group arrangements. These groups do feasibility studies, give advice on mergers of personnel and hospitals, and facilitate these changes. Most of these health experts have had no more experience organizing multispecialty groups, physicians, hospital organizations, and medical service organizations than the doctors who have worked in these arrangements.

# Chapter 9
# Malpractice Scandal

Whether or not doctors leave medicine, they might still face malpractice suits down the road. They must think about protecting their assets, because one suit could wreck even the most thoughtful doctor's future plans.

Although medical mishaps do occur, some suits are frivolous. I remember one morning while I was seeing patients in my office, my secretary told me that the sheriff was in my waiting room. I could only imagine what my patients were thinking when the sheriff walked in and insisted he had to serve me personally with some papers. When I read the papers, I learned I was being sued by Charlie Smith, on whom I had operated years ago.

I had evaluated Mr. Smith for severe back pain. Since all of his tests had been negative and he had lost twenty pounds, I thought we should get a bone scan. When Mr. Smith asked about the test, I told him I was checking his skeletal system for evidence of metastatic lesions or growths. He then asked if I was looking for cancer. I told him that it should be considered as a possibility. The bone scan was negative and Mr. Smith responded to conservative therapy. Three years later, he sued me over the mental anguish caused by his worries that he might develop cancer. As frivolous as this suit was, I still had to give a deposition, spend time with a lawyer, and go to my trial at the arbitration hearing. I won the case, but I have had to explain to every HMO since then why I was sued and why this suit shows up on my claim experience.

Patients are not the only ones who have filed frivolous suits against me. Three of my patients claimed to have been injured on the job and were trying to have their medical expenses covered by workmen's compensation insurance. All three of these patients shared the same lawyer. They complained to me often that he was unavailable, that he was moving too slowly on their cases, and that they were not receiving disability payments from their workmen's compensation insurance carrier. Since this lawyer had sent these patients to another neurosurgeon for a second opinion about how I was managing their cases, I suggested that they seek a second opinion about how he was managing their cases. One patient went back to the lawyer and embellished the conversation by telling the lawyer that I called him a jackass. The lawyer promptly sued me for malicious interference with a lawyer-client relationship. Before the trial began, the patient who embellished the conversation died of a myocardial infarction on his wedding night. At the trial, when I was on the stand and was asked whether or not I had called the lawyer a jackass, I replied that I never called him a jackass, but that I did believe him to be one. The judge and jury laughed and the judge threw the case out as a frivolous suit. I then countersued the lawyer for filing a frivolous suit and won my case, but the proceeds all went to pay my legal expenses, as these were not covered by my malpractice insurance.

The malpractice problem is a nationwide epidemic. Currently, American citizens, municipalities, and organizations are forced to pay high insurance rates to protect themselves against such liability claims. In the United States, these insurance payments total $80 billion a year (Huber,

1988). Out of this $80 billion, the legal profession nets an estimated 50 percent in fees. No other country in the world has such a liability system.

Legal experts state that tort law, or "the law of accidents and personal injuries" (Huber, 1988), was initially conceived to protect the life and limb of human beings and to help injured victims recover damages. Unfortunately, tort law has failed to do these things and, instead, has increased the price of services and goods for everyone. If tort law is unable to find the culprit, it now finds someone nearby with deep pockets.

During this process, liability insurance has not only become more expensive, but it has become virtually unavailable in some areas. As a result of this scarcity, small business owners and small businesses have suffered. The tort system of law hurts most those who have the least and does not provide a reliable safety net for its victims (Huber, 1988). Furthermore, tort law impedes innovation and weakens the competitive edge. The fear of potential liability suits has made companies reluctant to try new drugs, new vaccines, and other new products. Because many of its rivals in Asia and Europe do not face such obstacles, the United States has certainly lost its competitive edge.

The tort system encourages a witch-hunt for defects in a product or service. After a period that featured numerous such suits, lawyers abandoned their quest for defective products. Instead, they began attacking defects in the way products are sold. The courts mandated that manufacturers must issue better warnings. Later on, when these suits became more difficult to win, lawyers started attacking the phrasing of the warnings. When liability lawyers encountered strong opposition in this area, they started suing for the way warnings were disseminated. When the dissemination issue became resolved and was no longer remunerative, the liability lawyers initiated suits declaring that the warnings might have been issued to the wrong people.

Legal absurdity reached still another notch when the Supreme Court allowed a lower court ruling to stand and refused to hear a case dealing with liability in a pharmaceutical case ("Congressional Liability," 1989). From 1940 to 1971, over two million pregnant women took the synthetic hormone diethyestilbestrol (DES) to prevent morning sickness. The Food and Drug Administration approved the use of this drug and over three hundred pharmaceutical companies marketed it. Only after the drug had been used for thirty years did doctors report cancer cases among the daughters of DES users.

Mothers of several thousand DES plaintiffs could not remember just what brand they had used. The lower courts then suspended the rule that plaintiffs must prove that defendants are liable, assumed that all DES pills were the same, and created a market-share test. In this way, damages would be assessed against all drug manufacturing companies in proportion to their share of the original sales. Unfortunately, this line of reasoning may extend far beyond DES and pharmaceutical companies.

Frequently, the government and various professional organizations have issued standards of professional conduct and manufacturing quality. The Food and Drug Administration has approved drugs and various products according to its standards. If a physician, or anyone else, violates these regulations, liability is implied. If a physician or pharmaceutical company abides by the rules, however, then the standards count for naught. These standards do not help physicians or professionals prove their innocence in any way (Huber, 1988).

Much to the chagrin of the attorneys who felt that liability insurance would last forever, the United States insurance industry has entered a crisis. Since so many judgments have been brought against insurance companies, they have been forced to raise their premiums and to decrease the availability of liability insurance. For example, some insurance companies lost a series of judgments when they covered different vaccines. When a swine flu vaccine became available, no insurance company would insure its manufacturers. Some liberal senators made speeches in Congress declaring that the insurance companies were not living up to their responsibilities. Senator Edward Kennedy accused the insurance companies of trying to defraud the people and of only covering products that were potentially less risky. Finally, after much wringing of hands, the U.S. Congress passed a law that substituted the U.S. Treasury for the insurance industry. The total payments made as a result of the swine flu vaccination program amounted to $86 million, which was sixty times the original estimate (Huber, 1988). Years after the vaccination program, forty-one lawsuits are still pending, asking for a combined total of $97 million.

The tort system of law has devastated the supply of insurance. As a result, long-term coverage or occurrence-type coverage has virtually disappeared. Occurrence insurance would protect a doctor or a corporation for an extended period of time regardless of when an accident happens or when a claim is filed. This coverage was replaced by what the insurance companies call "claims-made" insurance. This insurance is not equal to the occurrence insurance and contains some strict limitations and stipulations. For instance, an insurance policy is sold on an annual basis and it is only good while the claim exists. If individuals do not carry continuous insurance, they are not covered. Should doctors wish to retire or should they die, they have to pay "tail coverage," which is usually four times the amount of the last premium. As a result of all the lawsuits that have been filed, the cost of insurance for contraceptive manufacturers, neurosurgeons, orthopedic surgeons, and obstetricians has increased and is less readily available. Historically, Lloyds of London has reinsured American insurance companies but, in 1985, this British consortium started pulling out of the American market (Huber, 1988). It felt that the United States was too risky a place in which to invest money. As a result of these events, the cost of malpractice insurance and liability insurance has skyrocketed over the past few years.

Tort lawyers have enabled plaintiffs to hide any additional insurance coverage that they might have. First-party insurance, such as health or automobile insurance, need not be revealed in tort lawsuits. As a result, plaintiffs can seek more compensation and the cost of the defendants' liability insurance increases. Tort lawyers have been able to persuade their colleagues in the federal government and state legislatures to pass laws virtually mandating that certain corporations, as well as certain professions, carry liability insurance in order to do business (Huber, 1988).

As Huber writes: "The whole point of insurance is to convert the random and unexpected into the regular and predictable" (1988). As a result of the changes that have occurred, the tort insurance system does exactly the opposite of what insurance was supposed to do in the first place.

Consumer activist Ralph Nader has proclaimed that the overwhelming causes of liability suits are malpractice, underwriting by insurance companies, and the weak disciplining of incompetent and negligent physicians by hospitals, medical societies, state licensing boards, and federal review agencies (1985). As some authorities have pointed out, Mr. Nader has overlooked the fact that it is not the incompetent doctors who are being sued, but rather the most highly trained physicians and surgeons who are performing the most difficult and sophisticated types of procedures (Mosberg, 1982, 1986). Stanley Schmidt states that "the underlying problem here is not an epidemic of incompetence among doctors. It is an epidemic of grossly unrealistic expectations of what doctors can do—encouraged, unfortunately by the courts which should know better. People have come to believe that doctors should never make mistakes, and courts have reinforced this absurd requirement of infallibility by punishing breaches with settlements way out of proportion to actual damages" (1984).

It has been noted that before 1978, there were only about 3.3 claims per 100 physicians filed each year. From 1978 through 1983, this figure reached 8 per 100 ("AMA Focuses Efforts On Liability Crisis," 1984). Opinions vary on the amount spent for defensive medical tests and procedures, but the best estimates are that between $15 billion and $30 billion a year is spent to avoid liability suits (Rust, 1985).

The liability crisis in America is also fueled by the contingency fee system. Champions of this system argue that contingency fees enable "small" plaintiffs access to the courts. Unfortunately, there is a direct relationship between contingency fees and expanded liability, all of which has increased the cost of most goods purchased and serviced. This situation injures the poor and the middle class, who can least afford this liability tax, when they are the ones it is supposed to help (Crovitz, 1989). Some observers feel that the litigious nature of the American public has created the present problem. A certain philosophy has permeated our society that no matter what happens, someone is responsible and must be forced to pay. Gest and Work state that "no longer is the decisive question whether the party sued—the defendant—has negligently harmed someone.

The question now centers on how much the plaintiff ought to be compensated for injuries" (1986).

Several solutions to this problem have been proposed. Peter Huber (1988) suggests that we return to the days of contractual law. He recommends that we make contracts ahead of time for most arrangements, and that if anything happens, this contract will be honored. He believes that since we have moved away from contractual law, tort law has been allowed to reign free. Unfortunately, contractual law might work in some areas of law, but it would not solve the issue with regard to medicine. A contractual arrangement already exists with workmen's compensation insurance. While a fee schedule is already in place, the problem still arises as to what constitutes an injury in the workplace. Richard Victor, executive director of Workers' Compensation Research Institute of Cambridge, Massachusetts, observes that in the past decade, workers' compensation rates have risen more than twice as fast as the general inflation rate. In 1986, compensation-related payouts reached an estimated $25 billion, more than three times the level a decade earlier (Emshwiller, 1989). The premiums for workers' compensation insurance have also tripled in the past ten years. One reason for this increase is that insurance companies settle 75 percent of disputed cases before trial, because they fear the unpredictability of the jury system. As a result, many people are compensated now for injuries, regardless of whether any accident really happened on the job (Emshwiller, 1989).

The American Association of Neurological Surgeons has recently testified before congressional committees and has made suggestions for medical malpractice reform. The AANS feels that Congress should expand the number of Alternative Dispute Resolution programs (ADR), that these programs should be binding, and that they should provide disincentives to bring any action in court after the ADR adjudicated the original claim. In other words, we should require any party that contests the ADR finding to pay the opposing party's litigation costs and attorney fees if the moving party loses at the trial or receives a smaller award. Furthermore, we should prohibit de novo review by the court. The access to the court should only be by way of appeal. There should be a certificate of merit required for each defendant, which would spell out the precise accusation against the defendant. This would help remove those named in a suit only because of their deep pockets. Any reform package should include specific requirements for an expert witness, such as that they be actively practicing and that they know the community standards. There should be creative ways to limit attorneys' fees. Awards for recovery from collateral sources should be reduced. Future medical care will be provided anyway, because all claimants will have some version of the national health care coverage that has been proposed. Furthermore, all payments of noneconomic damage should end upon the death of the individual. We should replace the Joint and Several Liability Rule with a comparative negligence rule. Defendants should be responsible for plaintiffs' damages according to their proportionate share of fault. We should also establish a more reasonable statute of limitations.. For example, there should be a maximum of two years from the date of discovery. Neonatal injuries should extend no further than six years. We should limit the noneconomic damage awards to $250,000 and completely eliminate the punitive damage from medical malpractice claims. I agree with the AANS's suggestions and would like to see them instituted.

# Chapter 10

# Professional Liability
# Situation in Annapolis

In the fall of 1993, I surveyed surgeons at the Anne Arundel Medical Center in my hometown of Annapolis, Maryland. I figured that other surgeons in the Annapolis area were facing malpractice problems similar to mine and wondered how they had protected themselves against pending lawsuits. I wanted to know how much malpractice insurance they carried, how many times they had been sued, and how well informed they were about protecting their assets. I asked forty-nine male surgeons the following ten questions and added my own responses to the study:

1. How many years have you been in practice?
2. How much malpractice insurance do you carry?
3. How many lawsuits have you defended?
4. How many are pending now?
5. Do you own your home with your wife?
6. Have you established a trust for your children?
7. Have you established a trust for estate purposes?
8. Have you transferred any assets to your wife or to your children?
9. Have you invested in annuities or other insurance products?

10. Have you taken any other steps to protect your assets?

I analyzed the pertinent results. I found that 92 percent of these physicians owned their homes as tenants in the entirety, while 6 percent of the doctors listed their homes in their own name. Only 2 percent of the physicians polled had transferred their homes completely to their wives, a figure resulting from my own inclusion in the survey. Tenancy in the entirety form of ownership is the most common form in the Annapolis area among surgeons. Very few physicians are the sole owners of their homes. Home ownership can be an emotional issue between marital partners and is usually resolved by a joint ownership arrangement. There is little risk to wife ownership, because most homes are awarded to the wife if there is a divorce.

I analyzed the relative number of malpractice suits the physicians had had filed against them. Twelve surgeons had defended one malpractice suit, eleven surgeons had defended two suits, ten surgeons had defended three suits, nine surgeons had defended four suits, six surgeons had defended five suits, and two surgeons had defended six suits. It is very common for surgeons to have at least one malpractice suit filed against them. Some had defended more suits than others because of their particular specialty. Neurosurgeons, obstetricians, and orthopedic surgeons are more likely to have more malpractice suits filed against them. In addition, the longer physicians practice, the more likely they are to be sued.

Ninety-six percent of the polled surgeons carried $1 million of liability insurance for one occurrence and $3 million of liability insurance per annum, whereas 4 percent had $2 million per occurrence and $5 million per annum. Surgeons routinely carried $5 million worth of liability insurance a few years ago and some even had $10 million. Now the large majority of the surgeons seem to feel that carrying $1 million of liability insurance per occurrence and $3 million per annum is sufficient, partly because the Maryland State Legislature enacted the $350,000 cap on pain and suffering. Being insured for $3 million may not be sufficient, however, because a patient may seek damages for lost income, which is a different matter altogether from pain and suffering. The 4 percent of the surgeons who carry $2 million worth of liability insurance are probably deluding themselves by thinking they are well protected.

Most of the surgeons surveyed had been in practice from five to twenty years. If I had interviewed a younger group, they would have had fewer malpractice suits. Younger physicians have had less time to be exposed to litigation and thus do not have as many suits brought against them. Conversely, if I had interviewed an older group, they would have defended more malpractice suits. Significantly, physicians who have been in practice twenty-five to thirty years have avoided the litigation explosion. Many of them are now retiring because of the huge malpractice premiums. If they see fewer patients or do only consultations, they cannot generate enough income to pay for their exorbitant malpractice premiums. Surgeons in their middle years, who are at the peak of their careers, are most likely to have more malpractice suits filed against them. Twenty surgeons in this survey had at least one suit pending against them. Forty-nine surgeons had established no trust for their wives or for their children. All fifty surgeons had invested in life insurance or annuities. I am the only surgeon who has taken additional steps to protect his assets.

What could the other surgeons do, whether they live in Annapolis or beyond? Ideally, each physician would carry at least $10 million worth of liability insurance. There is no substitute for affordable and available liability insurance. Unfortunately, liability insurance is neither readily available nor very affordable. It is mandatory in most hospitals, however, that practicing physicians carry a certain amount of insurance, normally $1 million.

# Chapter 11
# Protecting One's Assets

There are several ways for doctors to protect their assets. First, it is important to understand the concept of "fraudulent conveyances." Whenever an asset is transferred, which has the resulting effect of impinging on the rights of the transferor's creditors, this action might be considered a fraudulent conveyance (Bankruptcy Judges, 1986, sec. 548 [a-d]). Both state law and the Federal Bankruptcy Code define a fraudulent conveyance as a transfer of assets with either actual intent to defraud creditors or a transfer for less than fair value if: (1) the transferor is insolvent at the time of the transfer; (2) the effect of the transfer is to render the transferor insolvent; or (3) the transferor is about to incur debts beyond his or her ability to pay (Bankruptcy Judges, 1986, sec. 548 [a-d]). Creditors either can have such conveyances set aside or choose to disregard them. They then can attach the assets that were transferred as if the transferor had retained these assets. A court will carefully scrutinize such a transaction if it were not made for fair value.

A fraudulent conveyance may also include payments, mortgages, pledges, the creation of liens, and other encumbrances on assets. In addition, collusive foreclosures or lawsuits resulting in judgments may fall into this category if they are suspect. Rarely is direct proof of intent to defraud creditors found, but rather creditors must prove constructive intent to defraud. Particularly suspect are gifts to family members or transfers that are made at a time when creditors are contemplated. These consignments usually occur shortly after a major lawsuit has been filed. Creditors will not be oblivious to transfers that are disproportionate to assets that remain after any transfer. Courts also suspect any transfers that are incomplete; that is, transfers that do not follow the proper legal form or transfers over which the transferor has not completely relinquished dominion and control. A purported gift of stock certificates that remains in the transferor's safe deposit box would certainly be attached, as would a transfer of real property under a deed that was not recorded.

In order to diminish the risk of an asset transfer being treated as a fraudulent conveyance, one should consider making actual sales to spouses and children for the fair value of that property. The payment for the asset could be made in the form of a long-term note with a fairly low interest rate. Such a note would be much less attractive to a creditor than would the asset that has been sold. Since consideration must be fair, it is important that any property that does not have a readily ascertainable market value be professionally appraised. Furthermore, any such note should be enforceable. Finally, the seller should not retain undue control over the asset being transferred.

The statute of limitations on setting aside or reaching assets that are the subject of fraudulent conveyances will vary from state to state. The Federal Bankruptcy Code provides a one-year statute of limitations, while most states provide longer periods of time of up to ten years (Bankruptcy Judges, 1986). Keeping this notion of fraudulent conveyances in mind, we can now propose various techniques of asset protection. If a person has made a complete transfer of an asset and the transfer is not a fraudulent conveyance, creditors generally cannot reach that asset. A physician's spouse would be the most obvious beneficiary of such a gift. If no concern exists about creditors, there are good estate planning reasons for placing some assets separately in the name of each spouse. But placing assets in the spouse's name requires careful consideration of his or her will. If the spouse receiving gifts dies first and wills his or her entire estate to the donor, the plan will be frustrated. The spouse's will should designate that assets that were the subject of gifts to persons other than the giver be placed in a trust for the giver's benefit during his or her lifetime, preferably after having named an independent trustee.

Unfortunately, divorce is a very common problem in the United States. Many more people have divorces than are sued for the limits of their liability insurance coverage. Depending on how doctors perceive the strength and stability of their marriages, they should transfer assets with caution. Even if there is a divorce, however, the wife usually retains the principal and primary home. A divorce court would generally not require the spouse to recover any such assets, although the court might order that the assets be partitioned or sold and that the proceeds be divided between the parties.

This general principle of allocating gifts encourages the creation and regular funding of trusts for children, even at a time when many of the tax incentives for such arrangements have been destroyed. The best plan would be to establish a regular pattern of transfers to a trust with an independent trustee named without permitting the transferor to benefit from the trust assets. A court would be suspicious of a sudden large transfer or any transfers made after creditor problems already existed.

Any individual with creditor concerns who anticipates

a gift of inheritance from his or her parents or other relatives should encourage the donor to place these assets in a trust, rather than giving them outright. While physicians cannot protect themselves from creditors by creating trusts for their own benefit, their relatives can establish such a trust with "spendthrift" provisions. This means that benefits cannot be attached for payment of a debt, and a specified independent trustee is permitted to make discretionary distributions to the physician. Such a trust can protect both income and principal from creditors while these properties remain in trust, but any distributions actually made lose that protection.

Some physicians, such as those who practice in Maryland, have the advantage of practicing in a state that recognizes tenancy by the entirety in both real and personal property. This is a form of ownership permitted only to spouses. Each spouse has an equal interest in the property. If one spouse dies, the entire property passes to the survivor by operation of law. Neither party can unilaterally destroy the tenancy. Because one party cannot sever this type of ownership, neither can the creditor of only one party. If, for example, a home is owned under these terms, a creditor of one spouse cannot attach it or force its sale.

Therefore, property that a married couple acquires in Maryland will automatically take this form of ownership at the original time of purchase unless alternate provisions are made. One or both spouses may also convert some other form of ownership into tenancy by entirety after the initial acquisition. There are risks associated with tenancy by entirety. The parties may divorce, and unless they agree otherwise, the assets may be ordered partitioned between them or sold with the proceeds divided. It may be possible for spouses holding their assets in tenancy by the entireties to enter into an agreement determining how the assets will

91

be handled if a divorce occurs. Although settlement agreements between husbands and wives are generally enforceable, there is no case law specifically dealing with that particular question. The most likely challenge to such an agreement would be the lack of any consideration passing to a spouse who had agreed to reconvey an interest in property. Upon entering into such an agreement, one has to be certain that there is a full disclosure of the assets involved and that each party is represented by counsel.

A second risk to this financial maneuver would be the unexpected death of one of the spouses. If the nondebtor dies, ownership of the asset reverts to the debtor. Since judgments last twelve years and can be renewed indefinitely for successive twelve-year periods, death can be a definite risk to this arrangement (Maryland Rules of Annotated Code, 1989, sec. 2-625).

Physicians tend to carry large amounts of life insurance to provide for their families upon their deaths. Because public policy favors widows and orphans, many states, including Maryland, have statutes that specifically exempt proceeds of life insurance from creditor claims. Thus, the income from a policy, which is payable to a spouse or children or to a trust established for them, cannot be attached by creditors of the insured. This protection extends to the cash or loan value as well as to the death benefit. A creditor cannot force someone to cash in a policy or to borrow against it to pay debts. This law enhances the attractiveness of purchasing annuities or single-premium insurance as an investment. Because there are tax and other consequences associated with withdrawing funds from these policies, such policies should be purchased only after careful analysis of their benefits and drawbacks. Funds actually withdrawn by the insured individual lose their protected status. For possible protection from estate tax as well as from creditors, insurance ownership could be placed in an irrevocable trust.

Many people believe that assets placed in retirement plans are sheltered from creditors, primarily because of the "anti-alienation" provisions of ERISA (Employee Retirement Income Security Act), which prevents a participant from assigning or conveying plan benefits as collateral for a loan (Employment Retirement Act, 1974, sec. 1056). However, courts would more likely consider plan assets as susceptible to the claims of creditors. The Federal Bankruptcy Code exempts plans from creditor claims only to the extent reasonably necessary to provide for the support of the debtor and his or her dependents (Bankruptcy Judges, 1986, sec. 522[d][19][E]). State courts will look at different considerations, such as the degree of the debtor's control over the plan. If the plan is funded entirely by employer contributions, if the employee is not in control of the employer, and if the plan contains spendthrift language and has an independent trustee, then the participant's interest is more likely to be protected (Amendments and Federal Judgeship, 1984, sec. 363 [a]). On the other hand, a self-trusteed corporate plan, particularly one held by a sole shareholder, is less likely to escape creditors.

Although there have been no recent cases involving a professional corporation in Maryland, in a recent Fourth Circuit Court of Appeals decision involving a regular business corporation, the court showed leniency toward the debtor (*McLean v. Central States*, 1985). In ruling that the debtor's interest in a thrift plan and stock ownership plan was not subject to creditors' claims, the court emphasized the ERISA anti-alienation provision as opposed to the more restrictive spendthrift law.

Since there is some question about whether assets in a retirement plan would be exempt from creditors' claims, it might be advisable to use cash or other assets in the plan to purchase a life insurance policy, which is clearly exempt from creditors' claims by statute. Any money actually withdrawn from a retirement plan can be attached by creditors. Persons of retirement age should consider electing to take payments in the form of an installment annuity. Monies received in this form would be much less attractive to a creditor than a lump sum distribution. Married participants should consider not waiving the right to have plan benefits paid as a qualified joint survivor annuity. The fact that a spouse must consent to a waiver of this benefit is also helpful, because it takes one more degree of control away from the participant. Payment in this form will also diminish the actual amount passing to the participant, because the sum will be determined providing payments to the spouse after the participant's death.

Physicians cannot protect themselves from professional liability claims by incorporating. Some states do exempt a professional from claims against other shareholders in the corporation. Maryland's professional corporation statute does not provide such an exemption (Corporations and Associations Article, 1989, sec. 5-101).

Even if claims of creditors do arise, all states allow debtors some exemptions against seizure of their property. Maryland allows the following exemptions (Courts and Judicial Proceedings, 1989, sec. 11-504):

1. $3,000 in cash or property of any kind.
2. Clothing, items necessary to practice one's profession, disability payments, and personal property worth no more than $500.
3. Interests in insurance policies and annuities.
4. Varying amounts of wages.

The exemptions otherwise provided for in the Federal Bankruptcy Code are not allowable to Maryland debtors, but there is an additional $2,500 allowance for any real or personal property.

If both spouses hold separate assets, it is important to keep them separate. Each spouse should keep records of his or her assets, including proof of the source of that asset. Spouses should maintain separate bank accounts into which they deposit income from separate assets.

We can best demonstrate the above information by examining different financial scenarios.

## Scenario 1

If a male physician loses a malpractice suit and has a judgment rendered against him for $5 million, his liability insurance will pay $1 million and leave him with a personal exposure of $4 million. If the physician has a personal net worth of $3 million, how many of his personal assets can he protect? Assuming that his house is valued at $500,000, his pension plan is valued at $1.5 million, and he holds $1 million in personal assets in his name, such as cash, stocks, bonds, real estate, limited partnerships, cars, and boats, how much can be sheltered?

### Net Worth

| | |
|---|---|
| House | $500,000 |
| Pension Plan | $1,500,000 |
| Personal Assets | $1,000,000 |

The house can be protected entirely if he has legally transferred ownership to his spouse prior to the alleged malpractice incident. If the pension plan has been totally invested in insurance products such as annuities, the entire amount can probably be protected. From his personal assets, $100,000 can be protected if he has transferred this amount to his children's educational trust. The remaining $900,000 is vulnerable unless he has it invested in illiquid investments, such as real estate partnerships, which he would lose, but which would give him some leverage. Money that he received from his parents could also be protected if it were placed in a trust.

## Scenario 2

This scenario duplicates the circumstances described above. This physician's home can be protected in Maryland because of joint ownership as tenants by the entirety. Half of the retirement plan can be protected because of an investment in annuities, but $750,000 is vulnerable because it is invested in the stock market. All of his personal assets are vulnerable, except for $250,000 in annuities.

## Scenario 3

Again following the above hypothetical situation, this physician's house is solely listed in his name and is therefore vulnerable. The retirement plan is totally invested in the stock market and can be attached in some states after a liability judgment. The personal stocks and bonds are also exposed to the liability judgment. The irrevocable trust in the event of death is not very helpful at this point.

## Scenario 4

Assume a similar situation once again. This physician is simultaneously getting a divorce and has lost a large malpractice suit. His wife will get half of their home ($250,000), half of the retirement plan ($750,000), and $500,000 of his personal assets. That which he has not sheltered in any way would be available to satisfy a malpractice suit, except for that part protected by state law in the event of bankruptcy.

## Scenario 5

This physician is dying from cancer. His will directs that all of his assets go to his estate. Since the couple owns the house, it will pass on to his wife, as will other items of joint ownership. The $1 million life insurance and the $1.5 million retirement plan will go to the estate, which will be lost to a large liability judgment.

## Scenario 6

This physician is also dying, but he left his assets to a trust. Unfortunately, he will lose his house, because it was held only in his name. He will also lose his personal assets, but the life insurance and the retirement plan will go to his trust and will not be attached.

## Recommendations

The best way to safeguard one's assets in a litigious environment is to carry adequate liability insurance. Unfortunately, it is difficult to define what adequate liability insurance is, because jury awards can be unpredictable and can far exceed this maximum coverage. Furthermore, liability insurance is neither available nor affordable in some areas of the country. Physicians have to consider alternative solutions in order to protect their families and their assets.

It is strongly recommended that doctors assiduously avoid making any fraudulent conveyances. All transfers of assets should be done legally and in a timely manner. One should seek legal advice prior to transferring any assets. All transfers should be completed prior to the filing of any malpractice suits. Pension plans should be fully funded, with a considerable portion of these plans including life insurance products and annuities.

Rather than owning a home outright, it would be preferable for a physician to own a home jointly with a spouse as tenants in the entirety. Furthermore, a physician should strongly consider having the home listed solely in the spouse's name. The titles of automobiles, boats, and other expensive items can be initially held by various members of the family or legally transferred to them at a later date. Substantial assets should be transferred to an educational trust for the children. All inheritances should be directed to the next generation.

Finally, it is recommended that physicians seek competent legal advice for estate planning, which includes establishing an irrevocable trust. This would protect an estate from a large liability judgment.

# Chapter 12
# Changing My Career

Although I have not set the date, I have decided to leave the active practice of neurosurgery and to enter the world of finance. I have been studying for the Series 7 and the Series 65 security examinations and plan to take these tests soon. I have been planning my future career with a large New York brokerage firm where I will work as a health care consultant, advising the firm on issues and investments related to health care. Because I have a graduate degree in finance, I feel confident that I can adapt to another field. After all, finance is not foreign to me—I have been managing my personal investments and pension plan for nearly a quarter of a century. Still, it is only natural to wonder how things will turn out. Will I be successful?

It seems quite helpful to draw on past experiences when starting a new career. For example, Barbara Brown of Odenton, Maryland, was a librarian and a government lawyer for thirteen years. She gave up these professions to do that which makes her happy—she now owns the Quilt Connection. Her background helped her start a new business, deal with the legal aspects, and research African-American quilting.

A career change can occur early in one's career and help with the rest of one's life. The renowned anesthesiologist John Bonica wrestled professionally as the "Masked

Marvel," which paid his medical school bills. Later in life he wrote *The Management of Pain.*

People in almost every field change careers frequently during a lifetime, having an average of seven careers. Those in medicine have been fortunate for many years to have been blessed with so much stability in the profession. Now it seems things have caught up, and just as there has been downsizing and restructuring in so many industries, medicine is no different If present trends continue and managed care continues to grow, there will likely be a surplus of 150,000 specialists in a few years. If so, many doctors will have to retrain to become primary-care doctors or change careers.

I feel that doctors do not have to completely divorce themselves from the past. They can become a composite of all their education, efforts, and experiences. Dr. Murdock Head was professor emeritus at George Washington University and established the Airlie Foundation Conference Center near Warrenton, Virginia. He directed its activities for more than thirty years. He had degrees in dentistry, medicine, and law. Dr. Head produced motion pictures and television documentaries through a film unit he founded, Airlie Productions. He moderated a television show, wrote medical and legal textbooks, and advocated physical fitness. While it was unfortunate that he was convicted of conspiring to bribe two members of Congress, he arranged seminars and instituted aerobics for inmates while serving ten months at Maxwell Field, Alabama. He won reinstatement to medicine and to law and acted as a consultant to several universities.

Whatever career I pursue or whatever path my colleagues choose, we as Americans still have to attack a major threat to our society. Many states have already begun changing the laws to reform the medical liability disgrace.

Unfortunately, the House Judiciary Committee recently turned out an amendment which will be a step backward for all but the trial lawyers. Malpractice lawyers want to keep the money rolling in, regardless of whom they hurt. Until the liability laws change, the United States cannot be economically competitive with other nations. We all have to get involved and elect people to legislative positions who will rectify this situation, as has been done in California and Indiana.

I will miss my patients, but if the present trends continue, they will no longer be my patients anyway but become either wards of the state with a national health service or participants in an HMO referred by a gatekeeper without any particular loyalty or allegiance. I will miss the exciting surgical breakthroughs and new treatments. I will miss the operating room and the thrill of performing successful brain and spinal surgery. I will miss the challenge of doing well that which my colleagues have successfully done before me.

Regardless of my choices or those of other doctors, changes will continue to sweep across medicine. Doctors will be needed in any health care system, but they need not remain in the same role. Opportunities arise in any changing situation and doctors will have to watch out for these opportunities and identify a niche that suits their temperament. By virtue of their training and education, doctors have several options in many fields.

There is one area in which doctors should establish themselves as the leaders. Doctors should strive to be advocates for their patients in order to prevent insurance companies and the government from rationing needed medical care. Doctors can also assume a position in the forefront of medical ethics. There, they can consider, for example, how much we as a society are willing to spend on underdeveloped neonates, malformed newborns, alcoholics who need liver transplants, heavy smokers who need heart and lung transplants, or elderly people who need cardiac bypass surgery or heart transplants. Medical ethicists also need to make choices about the high medical costs that result from public health problems such as obesity, smoking, alcoholism, drug addiction, crime, and motor vehicle accidents.

The problem of providing long-term health care to the terminally and chronically ill has yet to be resolved in the United States. Doctors are involved in decisions in this area and should lead the movement to achieve results. Presently, this care is provided in private homes with the help of family members and friends. Some people can afford home nursing care, which consists of sitters and various grades of nursing. Medicare does not pay for custodial care in a nursing home and has a strict definition of skilled care for which it will pay up to approximately 80 percent for about one hundred days. As a result of third-party pressure, a new classification of subacute care is developing to replace some of the acute care days in hospital care. With the graying of America, the problem of what to do with Mom and Pop will only intensify as the pressure mounts for more budget cuts, particularly entitlement reductions.

As doctors face the wave of changes in medicine, it might help them to reflect on why they entered medicine in the first place. I personally decided on a medical career by the eighth grade. I wanted a career contributing to society where I would have a certain degree of autonomy. My years of training as an intern and a resident only confirmed my thoughts. I saw firsthand how government medicine could work when I served in the U.S. Army, first at Fort Polk, Louisiana, then the Ninety-first Evacuation Hospital in

Vietnam, and finally at Kimbrough Army Hospital at Fort Meade, Maryland. I also worked at the Birmingham Veterans Administration Hospital. I did not enjoy working under that socialized system, but endured, knowing that it would not last forever. Now that I have practiced neurosurgery for over twenty years as my own boss, I would have difficulty punching a clock or getting permission from an employer to take the day off.

The preparation for a career is a lifetime occupation in itself; it should be viewed as the acquisition of education, which in turn prepares us to deal with our family and our country. It also aids us in our thinking so that we can be analytical and creative with our decisions, in our writings, and in other forms of expression. Those of us who are so positioned as to have that choice of careers are able to make a difference and able to express that inner character manifested by the individual personality.

It seems to me that I have to remain in charge of my life and I suspect I will find a way to continue to have this choice. It may be that I will supplement medicine with some of the many options to which I have referred. Even though I may not be actively practicing medicine, I still look forward to its future and find the many new developments in spine surgery to be exciting. I anticipate even more developments in the years to come and hope to be able to participate in these new advances.

In the final analysis, the shape of American medicine will be determined by the government. We need not feel out of control as we confront this prospect, because we have more of a say in our government than we might think. As Bart Giamatti wrote in 1988: "Government is not the enemy, and neither are the people who elect governments. If we elect those who play on the forces that divide us, who play to our fears, we court a tragedy we may not be able to contain. And if we continue to elect those who denigrate what they pursue, who insist they are outsiders as they claw their way to the inside, we ought to ask if it is in our common interest to buy any more snake oil."

# Epilogue

# More Than Covered Lives: A Health Care Plan for the United States

Most Americans and politicians would agree that the United States has the best health care in the world and also would agree that something has to be done to change the way it is financed. None of the health care reforms thus far proposed have proved to be politically viable. Now that we have a new Congress, perhaps some sort of compromise arrangements can be realized. We propose a new and different health financing system that would provide coverage for all Americans and would still allow them flexibility and choice.

More than a third of the United States population is now covered by managed-care health plans, including health maintenance organizations (HMOs) and preferred provider organizations (PPOs). While these plans cover a growing share of the population and attempt to hold the line on the growth of health care costs, managed care may not take into account that health care consists of more than covered lives. If diversity and choice are to be maintained, managed care cannot be the sole cure-all for the health care system. First, substantial elements of managed care have depended on cost shifting. If everyone is in managed-care systems or in government price-control systems, then there is no potential for shifting costs. There are additional managed-care issues from the providers' perspectives. Capitation payment systems may limit testing and surgery and rely heavily on the "gatekeeper system," causing some care to be rationed. Managed-care systems may attempt to contract only with doctors, hospitals, and other providers on the basis of their economic credentials, meaning that they do not order a lot of tests and procedures. Managed-care plans may exclude some doctors without due process or deny some forms of accepted medical treatment. Some HMOs discriminate against doctors who serve minorities in the inner city. Thus, a viable health financing plan for the country requires a broader base than just extensions out of current managed-care systems.

Our proposed health care system combines Republican and Democratic tenets. It is based on a continued private-public mix of ownership and control of health care resources and delivery, which could continue to be for profit or not for profit, and it features diverse sources of health care financing. This is a universal coverage plan, which would entitle every American citizen and legal resident to a universal health care card. It would settle divisive issues such as preexisting illnesses, portability, employer mandates, and preferential tax deductions. This plan would be utilitarian in that the government could finance care for the poor, and yet it would be libertarian in that those households which choose to do so could purchase additional health care.

This health plan starts with removal of the tax deductions for employer-purchased health insurance. Members of Congress are currently discussing proposals to modify the Internal Revenue Code. This change would also disembarrass employers of paying for health insurance, which interferes with American competitiveness in the international economy. The national health insurance plan would give participants a choice of either an indemnity insurance carrier or a managed-care HMO. Furthermore, participants would know that all services are supplied by participating providers at prenegotiated rates. As opposed to health insurance in the private sector, the national health insurance plan would rebate a prorated amount of their premium if their benefits were not fully utilized. It would settle the issue of insurance portability, because workers could purchase insurance themselves and retain it when they change jobs. Households would have a choice of ways to finance their health care. They could pay out of pocket, purchase private indemnity insurance, or obtain managed-care coverage. Rather than having predominantly employment-based private group insurance or only government financing we recommend the following changes:

- Health insurance payments would not be tax deductible and would be based on reported household income.
- Preexisting diseases, community and experience ratings, and portability would no longer be factors since there would be universal coverage.
- Payment for the health care credit card would be based on household income level and size. Whereas a husband and wife without children would pay $4500 per year ($375 per month) for this health care, a family with children would pay more and a single person would pay less.
- All citizens and legal residents would receive a health insurance credit card. For example, a household with a husband and wife would use the card to receive health care purchased with the annual

$4,500 ($375 per month) health insurance premium, as well as the major-medical insurance benefits with limits up to $100,000.

- A husband and wife with an income of $35,000 or more could purchase private insurance, either indemnity or managed care, and indicate this choice on their tax return with proof. Alternatively, they could participate in the government-sponsored health insurance program and receive a prorated rebate if they did not fully utilize their benefits. This rebate could take the form of cash or the credit could be applied toward their income taxes the following year. The household would get the rebate rather than each person.

  A husband and wife with an income less than $35,000 would pay only $2,500 per year ($208 per month) for their $4,500 policy and a $100,000 major-medical insurance policy. This group could also choose whether it wanted its care provided by indemnity insurance or the managed-care system that participates with the government plan. Although the husband and wife would still receive $4,500 of health insurance benefits and the $100,000 major-medical insurance policy, their rebate would be prorated based on the $2,500 payment.

The third tier of the system would provide health coverage for households that have income below the federal poverty level. These households would be insured under the government-sponsored managed-care system and would not be eligible for any rebate. Importantly, this plan would separate health care financing from welfare payments for low income households, providing motivation to enter the job market while retaining health care financing.

Although any universal health care plan will incur increased costs, the government could increase its revenues and finance this plan by:

1. Eliminating the tax deductibility of employer-purchased health insurance.
2. Receiving increased taxes from the wage increases that many employees would receive from their employers in lieu of health insurance.
3. Receiving revenues from premium payments for government-sponsored health insurance policies.
4. Abolishing Medicare and the acute part of Medicaid. (However, one area of government revenue would be reduced, as there would no longer be a Medicare supplemental tax of 1.25 percent on income.)
5. Abolishing other federal and state health programs for specific conditions, such as end-state renal disease.
6. Transforming the Veteran's Administration Hospital system into geriatric acute-care facilities and long-term health care centers for the anticipated increased number of people receiving these services.

This health care plan would save the American public and businesses millions of dollars. For example, individuals would no longer need medical insurance as part of their automobile insurance policy. The medical care component of workmen's compensation insurance could be deleted, reducing another cost of employment to business. In addition, medical malpractice awards would be reduced.

Beyond issues of health care financing lie matters of decision-making. Presently, the state insurance commissioners do not uniformly guarantee that health insurance companies provide the contracted benefits. The health insurance companies and managed-care providers under this plan would need to be monitored more effectively by a national insurance commissioner and agency.

Additionally, there cannot be broad health care reform unless there is a concommitant medical malpractice reform. In recent congressional testimony, the American Association of Neurological Surgeons listed the following suggestions for medical malpractice reform:

- Congress should expand the number of Alternative Dispute Resolution programs that should be binding and provide disincentives to bring court action after the ADR adjudicates.
- De novo review by the court should be prohibited, with the only access to the court being by way of appeal.
- Each defendant should have a Certificate of Merit. This would help those sued only because of their "deep pockets."
- Any reform package should include specific requirements for expert witnesses; for example, they should be in active practice and know the community medical standards.
- We need caps on the amount of money involved in malpractice suits. There should be creative ways to limit attorney fees. There should also be a reduction of awards for recovery from the collateral sources; future medical care will be provided anyway, because all claimants will have national health coverage. All payments of non-economic damage should end with the individual's death. We should limit non-economic damage awards to $250,000 and elim-

inate the punitive damage for medical malpractice claims. We should replace the Joint and Several Liability rule with a Comparative Negligence rule; each defendant should be responsible for a plaintiff's damages according to the proportionate share of the fault. We should also establish a more reasonable statute of limitations. For example, there should be a maximum of two years from the date that the alleged negligence was discovered. Neo-natal injuries should not extend beyond six years.

This broad health financing plan provides universal coverage and allows more Americans to participate in their health decision–making with positive, rather than perverse, incentives for rational cost consciousness. Many households will opt out of the national health insurance plan. Some will choose to stay in the government-sponsored plan, with increased information regarding the cost of their health care decisions and with the ability to select an indemnity or a managed-care system. While the issue of health care is still in the mind of America, we feel there is room for compromise with this plan.

—Jack Kushner, M.D.
—Rose Rubin, Ph.D.,
Professor of Economics,
University of Memphis

# References

"AMA Focuses Efforts On Liability Crisis." *AMA News,* July 27, 1984, 4.

Amendments and Federal Judgeship Act of 1984, Sec. 363(a), 11 U.S.C. Sec. 541(c)(1) 1984.

Arnett, Grace-Mani. "Cops and Doctors: It May Take a National Police Force to Monitor the Clinton Health Plan." *The Washington Post,* Dec. 19, 1993, C2.

Balagot, Maiza. *Leaving the Bedside.* Chicago: American Medical Association, 1992, 118.

Bankruptcy Judges, United States Trustee and Family Farmer Act of 1986, Sec. 283(i), 11 U.S.C. Sec. 522(d)(10)(E)(1986).

Bird, Caroline. *Second Careers: New Ways to Work After 50.* Boston: Little, Brown, 1992, 357.

"Congressional Liability." *The Wall Street Journal,* Nov. 2, 1989, 18.

Corporations and Associations Article of the Annotated Code of the Public General Laws of Maryland. 1989 Replacement Volume, Sec. 5–101, et. seq.

Courts and Judicial Proceedings Article of the Annotated Code of the Public General Laws of Maryland. 1989 Replacement Volume, Sec. 11–504(a)(5).

Crovitz, L. G. "Contingency Fees and the Common Good." *The Wall Street Journal,* July 21, 1989, A14.

Curry, Wesley, ed. *Roads to Medical Management: Physician Executives' Career Decisions.* Tampa, FL: American College of Physician Executives, 1988.

Employment Retirement Income Security Act of 1974, Sec. 206(d)(1), 29 U.S.C. Sec. 1056(1974).

Emshwiller, J. R. "Small Firms Find Workers' Compensation to

Be Painful." *The Wall Street Journal,* June 22, 1989, B2.

Felsenthal, Ed. "Doctors Seek Right to Join Forces to Negotiate with Health Plans." *The Wall Street Journal,* Jan. 3, 1994, 12.

Ferrari, B. T. "Group Practices: Staying Open to Surprises." In *Roads to Medical Management,* Wesley Curry, ed. Tampa, FL: American College of Physician Executives, 1988, 68–73.

Fortrin, Gilles. Personal conversation with Pam Politer cited in *Research Analyst,* Canada's Department of National Health and Welfare, Idlewilde, Ontario, July 8, 1993.

Gest, T., and C. P. Work. "Sky-High Damage Suits." *U.S. News & World Report,* January 27, 1986, 35–43.

Giamatti, A. Bartlett. *A Free and Ordered Space.* New York: W. W. Norton, 1988, 124.

Goldstein, Amy. "Health Reform: How Doctors See It." *Washington Post,* Jan. 3, 1994, A1, A8–9.

Goodman, John C., and Gerald L. Musgrave. *Patient Power: Solving America's Health Care Crisis.* Washington, D.C.: Cato Institute, 1992.

Griffitts, Jack. *Call Me a Doctor.* Arlington, VA: The American Spectator, 1991.

Huber, P. W. *Liability: The Legal Revolution and Its Consequences.* New York: Basic Books, 1988.

Jeakle-Hill, Catherine. *Bulletin of American College of Surgeons* 78, no. 7 (Sept. 1993): 13–18.

Jones, Frederic. "Study Tour Examines Health Care Systems in Germany, Holland: Part Two: The German System." *Physician Executive* 19, no. 5 (Sept. 1993): 58.

Kabany, N. Cited in S. Peres, *The New Middle East.* New York: Henry Holt, 1993, 64.

McIntosh, David. "Without Malpractice Reform, Forget Health Care Reform." *Wall Street Journal,* Sept. 22, 1993, A21.

*McLean v. Central States S. & S. Areas Pen. Fund* 762 F. 2nd 1204 (CA 1985).

Markey, James P., and William Parks. "Occupational Change: Pursuing a Different Kind of Work." *Monthly Labor Review,* Sept. 1989, 3–12.

Maryland Rules of the Annotated Code of the Public General Laws of Maryland. 1989 Replacement Volume, Sec. 2–625.

Morain, Claudia. "Is There Life after Private Practice?" *American Medical News*, Aug. 17, 1992, 41–45.

Mosberg, W. H., Jr. "Tort Reform—Now!" *Neurosurgery* 10 (1982): 133–40.

——. "The Liability Insurance Crisis." *Neurosurgery* 19 (1986): 857–84.

Nader, R. "Maybe Malpractice Is One Cause of Malpractice Suits." *Baltimore Evening Sun*, Sept. 11, 1985, A13.

Pasov, Joseph M. "The Course Doctor." *Golf Illustrated*, April 1992, 55–57.

Pear, Robert. "Doctors Planning Battle against Health-Care Plan." *New York Times*, June 15, 1993, A20.

Politer, Pam. *Bulletin of American College of Surgeons* 78, no. 9 (Sept. 1993): 13–18.

Prewo, Wilfried. "Germany Is Not a Model." *Wall Street Journal*, February 1, 1994, A14.

Rucker, T. Donald, and Martin D. Keller, eds. *Careers in Medicine: Traditional and Alternative Opportunities.* Garret Park, MD: Garret Park Press, 1986, 223–45.

Rust, M. "Data Problem Stymies Tort Reform." *AMA News*, March 8, 1985, 2, 31–32.

Salerno, S. "High Price of Managed Care." *The Wall Street Journal*, Jan. 18, 1994, A16.

Schmidt, S. "Infallibility Required." *Analog. Science Fiction/Science Fact*, June 1984, 6–11.

Smallwood, Karen G., and C. N. Wilson. "Physician-Executives Past, Present and Future." *Southern Medical Journal* 85, no. 8 (Aug. 1992): 840–44.

Tregarthen, Suzanne. "Statistics Overstate Health-Care Costs." *Wall Street Journal*, Aug. 18, 1993, A10.

U.S. General Accounting Office: Report to the Chairman, House of Representatives. Canadian Health Insurance—Lessons for the United States. GAD/HRD-91-90, Washington, D.C. June 1991.

115

"Vaccine Compensation Update and Review." *The Executive Letter.* New York: Insurance Information Institute, Sept. 8, 1986, 2–3.

Ward, Aileen. *John Keats: The Making of a Poet.* New York: Farrar, Straus and Giroux, (1963) 1986, 459.

Weil, T. P. "The German Health-Care System: A Model for Hospital Reform in the United States?" *Hospital and Health Service Administration* 37, no. 4 (1992): 540.

Wilke, Richard. "Practice Mobility among Young Physicians." *Medical Care* 29, no. 10 (Oct. 1991).

Winslow, R. "HMO's Are Expected to Deliver Strong Profit Growth." *The Wall Street Journal,* Jan. 18, 1994a, B4.

———. "In Health Care, Low Cost Beats High Quality." *The Wall Street Journal,* Jan. 18, 1994b, B1.

Winslow, R., and E. Felsenthal. "Physicians Fight Back as Insurers Cut Them from Health Network." *The Wall Street Journal,* Dec. 30, 1993, A1, A5.

www.ingramcontent.com/pod-product-compliance
Lightning Source LLC
Chambersburg PA
CBHW051430280526
45785CB00003B/1237